The Gig Economy

The Gig Economy

A Critical Introduction

Jamie Woodcock
Mark Graham

polity

First published in 2020 by Polity Press

Polity Press
65 Bridge Street
Cambridge CB2 1UR, UK

Polity Press
101 Station Landing
Suite 300
Medford, MA 02155, USA

ISBN-13: 978-1-5095-3635-1
ISBN-13: 978-1-5095-3636-8 (pb)

A catalogue record for this book is available from the British Library.

Typeset in 11 on 13 pt Monotype Bembo by Servis Filmsetting Ltd, Stockport, Cheshire
Printed and bound in the UK by CPI Group (UK) Ltd, Croydon

The publisher has used its best endeavours to ensure that the URLs for external websites referred to in this book are correct and active at the time of going to press. However, the publisher has no responsibility for the websites and can make no guarantee that a site will remain live or that the content is or will remain appropriate.

Every effort has been made to trace all copyright holders, but if any have been overlooked the publisher will be pleased to include any necessary credits in any subsequent reprint or edition.

For further information on Polity, visit our website: politybooks.com

Contents

Figures and tables

Figures

Table

Acknowledgements

We would first like to thank George Owers for commissioning and then supporting the book throughout the whole process, as well as Julia Davies and the rest of the team at Polity. We would also like to thank our three anonymous reviewers for their critical and constructive feedback. We are very grateful to Adam Badger who worked with us to source background material for the book and provided many insights and suggestions along the way. Adam is a wonderful colleague to work with on this sort of project. Thanks as well to David Sutcliffe for his extensive editorial support and always sharp suggestions, and to Ian Tuttle for his careful copyediting.

Giorgio Marani patiently worked with us on many drafts to get figure 1 just right, and we appreciate his skill and attention to detail in the final product. The fantastic illustrations in the final chapter were made by John Philip Sage. Thank you for visualizing the futures we hope to travel towards.

We owe an important thanks to the German Federal Ministry for Economic Cooperation and Development (BMZ) and the Deutsche Gesellschaft für Internationale Zusammenarbeit (GIZ), as well as the ESRC (ES/S00081X/1) for supporting our research in this area. We would like to acknowledge also the Leverhulme

Prize (PLP-2016-155), the European Research Council (ERC-2013-StG335716-GeoNet), and The Alan Turing Institute (EPSRC grant EP/N510129/1) for their ongoing support.

The book has drawn on previous and ongoing research projects at the Oxford Internet Institute. We are particularly thankful to the Fairwork team, including Sandy Fredman, Paul Mungai, Richard Heeks, Darcy du Toit, Jean-Paul van Belle and Abigail Osiki on the South African project; Balaji Parthasarathy, Mounika Neerukonda and Pradyumna Taduri in India; Sai Englert, Adam Badger and Fabian Ferrari in the UK; as well as Noopur Raval, Srujana Katta, Alison Gillwald, Anri van der Spuy, Trebor Scholz, Niels van Doorn, Anna Thomas and Janine Berg – many of whom also discussed the ideas and offered feedback on the manuscript. We also owe a debt of gratitude to our brilliant colleagues at the Oxford Internet Institute who apply a critical lens to digital work and the gig economy. We especially wish to thank Amir Anwar and Alex Wood for the many collaborations and conversations that have shaped our thinking on this topic. But we also acknowledge the rest of our research cluster for collectively building a research environment so conducive to critical, innovative and engaged research into the digital economy. Thank you to Sanna Ojanperä, Michel Wahome, Sai Englert, Adam Badger, Martin Dittus, Joe Shaw, Margie Cheesman, Marie-Therese Png, Fabian Braesemann, Chris Foster, Stefano de Sabbata and Ralph Straumann.

In addition, we would like to thank Phil Jennings, Abigail Hunt, Sanna Ojanperä, Nick Srnicek, Alessandro Gandini, Callum Cant, Wendy Liu, Robert Ovetz, Darcy du Toit, Sandy Fredman, Marc Thompson and Jason Moyer-Lee for taking the time to read an earlier draft of this book and for offering their incredibly valuable insights and feedback on the manuscript. Any faults or omissions are of course only our own. We are grateful to the role played by Antonio Casilli and ENDL in building a community of scholars focused on digital labour: a community that provided a fertile group for discussions that shaped this book. We would also both like to acknowledge Six Silberman and Christina Colclough for their support and friendship over the last few years. It has inspired and shaped much of the work we do.

Jamie would like to thank Lydia for her continuing and invaluable support, both in general and with more book writing projects. He would also like to thank the editors of Notes from Below who offered feedback as well as ongoing theoretical and practical inspiration. Callum Cant's *Riding for Deliveroo* (which is due to be published at the same time as this book) has been an important influence on making sense of the gig economy from the perspective of workers. Mark would like to thank his family. Jean Graham for raising a family whilst working in the gig economy. Thanks for your endless support to all of us despite all the challenges you have encountered as a precarious worker. And thanks to Kat: for always being a steady source of wisdom, advice and good humour – no matter how difficult a day of work has become.

Finally, we would like to thank all of the workers we have spoken to and whose voices we have tried to feature within the book. Ultimately, this is a book about hope for fairer futures of work. As such, we dedicate it to the workers whose stories are not already written.

Introduction

Everybody is talking about the gig economy. From newscasters to taxi drivers to pizza deliverers to the unemployed, we are all aware of the changes to our jobs, our professions, our economies and our everyday lives wrought by the gig economy. There are now an estimated 1.1 million people in the UK working in the gig economy, delivering food, driving taxis and offering other services – this is as many people as work for the National Health Service (Balaram et al., 2017). Eleven per cent of workers in the UK have earned income from working on digital labour platforms (Huws and Joyce, 2016), while 8 per cent of Americans worked on a 'gig' platform in 2016, rising to 16 per cent for the 18–29 age bracket (Smith, 2016). An increasingly common feature of the gig economy is the use of digital labour platforms – tools that allow employers to access a pool of on-demand workers. It is predicted that by 2025, one-third of all labour transactions will be mediated by digital platforms (Standing, 2016). Around the world, the number of people who have found work via platforms is estimated to be over 70 million (Heeks, 2017). Even more headline-grabbing are the numbers released in a 2015 study by McKinsey:

Up to 540 million people could benefit from online talent platforms by 2025. As many as 230 million could find new jobs more quickly, reducing the duration of unemployment, while 200 million who are inactive or employed part time could gain additional hours through freelance platforms. As many as 60 million people could find work that more closely suits their skills or preferences, while an additional 50 million could shift from informal to formal employment. (Manyika et al., 2015)

We have written this book as a critical introduction for those who want to find out more about how work is changing today. Throughout the book we draw on examples from our own research, stories from workers themselves, and the key debates in the field. Work is not just an interesting concept or debating point, but also something that most of us have to do. The conditions under which we find and undertake work can therefore tell us much about society around us – including issues of power, technology and who benefits in the economy. We wrote this book as engaged researchers, not only to document the rise of the gig economy, but also to critically explore how it is being changed right now by both workers and platforms, as well as how it could be transformed in future.

The focus of this book is on the precarious and fractured forms of work that have become known as 'gigs' (that is casual, piecemeal work) within the so-called 'gig economy'. These include things like delivery, taxis and domestic work. We also focus specifically on platform work, in which gigs are mediated digitally via platforms like Uber and Deliveroo. While 'gigs' have always existed across many sectors of the economy, the gig economy enabled by digital platforms is growing rapidly, and increasingly replacing non-platform gig work. By focusing on the platform, we can begin to understand how other kinds of precarious work are being reshaped, but also how this has already begun to affect the rest of the economy. In other words, we are in an important historical moment: one in which we are witnessing an unprecedented normalization of the platform-based labour model. It is therefore crucial to not just describe it, but also to shape it so that it can become more just and fair.

What do we mean by the gig economy?

The 'gig' in the term 'gig economy' refers back to the short-term arrangements typical of a musical event. An aspiring musician might celebrate getting a gig, or tell a friend that they have got a gig in the back room of a pub or other venue. This is of course no guarantee that they will get to perform regularly. There might be the chance of a repeat performance if they play particularly well, or are particularly popular – or it may just be a one-off. They might get paid – either a fixed fee, a share of the ticket price, or payment in kind (some free drinks perhaps). Their expenses might get covered. But also, they might not.

There are clearly some parallels here with the work we have already discussed. The tasks that underpin the gig economy are also typically short, temporary, precarious and unpredictable, and gaining access to more of them depends on good performance and reputation. However, work in the gig economy, as we will show, is very different to musical gigs. With much gig work, there is little possibility of career advancement – particularly if you are stuck doing endless tasks rather than 'a job'. What the term 'gig economy' captures is an economic transformation in which work in many sectors is becoming temporary, unstable and patchworked. It entails workers spending less time at one job, a risk of time spent without income, workers undertaking more jobs (possibly at the same time), and unpaid time spent searching for tasks or gigs.

In this book, we use the term 'gig economy' to refer to labour markets that are characterized by independent contracting that happens through, via, and on digital platforms. The kind of work that is offered is contingent: casual and non-permanent work. It may have variable hours and little job security, involve payment on a piece-work basis, and lack any options for career development. This relationship is sometimes termed 'independent contracting', 'freelancing' or 'temporary work' ('temp' for short). While the term has traditionally been used to refer to a broader range of activities that happen in both digitally mediated and non-mediated ways (such as bike messengers and cab drivers), we focus in this book on digital platforms because of the scale they involve. The platform is the digital base upon which the gig firm is built. It provides 'tools to bring together the supply of, and demand for, labour' (Graham and Woodcock, 2018: 242), including the app, digital infrastructure and algorithms for managing the work. As Nick Srnicek (2017: 48) has argued:

> Platforms, in sum, are a new type of firm; they are characterized by providing the infrastructure to intermediate between different user groups, by displaying monopoly tendencies driven by network effects, by employing cross-subsidization to draw in different user groups, and by having designed a core architecture that governs the interaction possibilities.

Platforms have become central to our social activities. They bring together users, capture and monetize data, as well as needing to scale to be effective. Indeed, they are now starting to mediate just about every imaginable economic activity, and they tend to do so through gig economy models. Many digital platforms have a low entry requirement and deliberately recruit as many workers as possible, often to create an oversupply of labour power, and therefore guarantee a steady supply of workers on demand to those who need them. In a world where people are talking about 'Uber' as a verb: 'the Uber for dog walking', 'the Uber for doctors', and even 'the Uber for drugs', it is important to understand both the histories and futures of this emerging – and increasingly normalized – model of work. The gig economy naturally has immediate effects on gig workers, but as it develops it will affect work more broadly in profound ways.

The rise of the 'gig economy' has become symbolic of the way that work is changing. The term refers to the increase in short-term contracts rather than permanent or stable jobs. It has been touted by many as offering much greater flexibility for workers, employers and customers, rather than the stifling nature of some traditional employment contracts. Employers can choose when and how they want to hire workers. And clients and customers can reap the benefits of this flexibility: getting food delivered quickly, hiring a web developer and ordering a taxi on demand has never been easier. Workers can supposedly choose what to do, how, when, where and for whom. Many are able to find jobs and income previously hard to obtain.

The gig economy, however, also has a dark side. Emerging evidence is pointing towards a range of negative outcomes for workers: low pay, precarity, stressful and dangerous working conditions, one-sided contracts and a lack of employment protection (Wood et al., 2019b). This can result in 'a raw deal' for workers, which in the US context can also be seen as an attempt to 'replace the New Deal' (Hill, 2017: 4). Some platforms have replaced previous kinds of work – for example, minicabs being replaced by Uber – whereas others are creating new kinds of jobs – the training of machine learning systems by image tagging and data entry, for instance. In all cases, existing working practices are being transformed. The so-called 'standard employment relationship' is being undermined through fragmented work and increased casualization. Activities that were previously considered to be a formal or standard job can be mediated through platforms to try and bypass rules, standards and traditions that have protected working standards. One example of this is the new platform being proposed for the UK's National Health Service that would have nurses bid for shifts under the guise of offering flexibility rather than being provided with more stable contracts.[1]

We focus on two kinds of work in this book. The first is what we refer to as 'geographically tethered work'. You may have used an app to order takeaway food, a taxi, or even someone to clean your house. This kind of work existed before digital platforms, and requires a worker to be in a particular place to complete the work – the pizza delivery person needs to transport a pizza from a particular kitchen to a particular house. What is new here is that the work process can now be organized over the internet, usually through an app. All over the world there are now delivery riders, taxi drivers, cleaners and care workers finding their work in this way. In some cases, these workers are highly visible, if we think of the brightly coloured uniforms of food delivery riders or the stickers on Uber drivers' windows. In other cases – such as home cleaning services – this is work that continues to be invisible to many, hidden behind the closed doors of the household. The second kind of work we focus on is 'cloudwork'. This refers to online freelancing, as well as shorter digital tasks called microwork. Online freelancing involves work that can be completed remotely, like web development, graphic design and writing that happen on platforms like UpWork or Freelancer. Microwork, on the other hand, involves much shorter tasks like image recognition and transcription that are typical on platforms such as Amazon Mechanical Turk. Both forms of work are organized digitally over the internet, with workers completing tasks remotely for the requesting organizations or individuals. Workers live all over the world, doing work that can come from anywhere.

The use of digital tools in gig work also makes many jobs increasingly invisible. While some platforms bring workers into contact with customers, others are obscured behind apps and websites. In many cases, this means we know little about the new experiences and challenges faced by gig economy workers. These issues are compounded in many industries and places by a huge oversupply of labour in the market. As a result of this oversupply, individual workers have very little power to negotiate wages or working conditions with their employers. It is this lack of power that workers have relative to their employers that is one of the reasons why workers in many industries have traditionally grouped together in trade unions. A group of workers is much better equipped to collectively negotiate with their employer, or other powerful actors in the value chains of work, than a single one is. Yet, in most countries, the existing trade union movement lacks effective strategies to organize gig workers.

As there are an increasing number of workers finding employment through platforms, the relative lack of collective voice for platform workers poses important questions about their ability to collectively organize and bargain with platforms and employers. There are exciting examples of new forms of worker organizing on platforms that offer geographically tethered work – for example, the Deliveroo struggles taking place across multiple European countries, or the attempts by platform delivery drivers across Africa and Asia to collectively demand better working conditions. The location-specific nature of this sort of work offers the opportunity for workers to come together, organize and collectively withdraw their labour. But it is worth remembering that much of what is done in the gig economy has very little co-presence in either time or space. Online freelancing jobs can just as easily be done next door or on the other side of the world. It is therefore less clear what forms organizing can take in those contexts.

This book considers some of the key social, economic and political implications of these transformations of work – providing an account of the development, debates and operation of the gig economy. These themes are then further explored by looking at the experience of gig workers themselves, as well as considering emerging forms of resistance and pathways towards less exploitative forms of work.

Why did we write this book?

Both authors have studied work, and workers, in the gig economy in various ways since the gig economy took off, including extended periods of on-the-ground research in the UK, the Philippines, Vietnam, Kenya, Nigeria, Ghana, Uganda, Rwanda, South Africa and India.[2] In addition to our qualitative and ethnographic fieldwork, we have carried out large-scale surveys, and mapped quantitative datasets that reveal global-scale patterns of trade in work through gig economy platforms. However, what has struck us most in our research on the gig economy are the stories from the workers themselves. These stories should be at the centre of any discussion about the transformation of work. We would like to start with two that have particularly stuck with us.

Jamie has been doing research with Deliveroo riders in London since June 2016: observing, interviewing and using forms of co-research in collaboration with workers. Delivering food is an example of 'geographically tethered' work. One of the riders, who had been a participant in Jamie's research since the beginning, told a particularly revealing story about the experience of working for Deliveroo. At the end of an interview, Jamie asked the driver what he thought the most challenging part of the work was. Expecting the driver to mention the low pay, insecure contracts or threat of accidents, he was instead told the following story. The driver worked at two other jobs in addition to Deliveroo. In the morning he would wake up and go to the first job, trying to eat breakfast before he left. Over lunch he worked a shift for Deliveroo, making sure to grab something quick to eat on the way. In the afternoon he worked at the third job, before starting the evening shift at Deliveroo. The most challenging aspect of the work was making sure he ate enough food once he got home to ensure he had the energy to get up and repeat the process the next day. Deliveroo is marketed as a service for delivering food to stylish young professionals, but the reality is that many of his deliveries were to people too exhausted from working to make their own dinner. This is especially ironic given how Deliveroo brands itself. His story is therefore a damning indictment of the realities of gig work in London: a worker struggling to eat enough calories to deliver food to people who are too tired from work to make their own.

Mark has been studying and speaking with cloudworkers in Sub-Saharan Africa since 2009. In 2017, he and his colleague Amir Anwar spoke to an online freelancer in Takoradi, a medium-sized city in Western Ghana, who primarily sourced work through Upwork.com.[3] The worker, a university graduate with a family to support, previously worked at a local firm in Takoradi. After doing some freelancing on Upwork at nights and weekends, he decided to take the plunge and quit his job in the local economy. He now completes a variety of tasks (including app testing, data entry, technical writing and search engine optimization). While these tasks are fairly varied, they have two things in common. First, they pay better than his previous job in Ghana. Second, he is rarely told what they are for, or why he is doing them. He knows, for instance, that he needs to write a short article on gardening. But isn't told why the client needs it or how they create value from it. While the pay is good, the pressures to deliver are extremely high. In the online freelancing world, reputation is everything and workers are terrified of not receiving a five-star review from clients. Reviews from people the worker does not know have become an important part of management in the gig economy. Compounding this issue is the sporadic nature of work. When contracts are obtained by workers, they often need to be carried out very quickly. As such, the worker we spoke to ended up working extremely long shifts. He described multiple 48-hour marathon working sessions without sleep, simply in order to not disappoint his clients. Despite these gruelling work conditions, he maintained a positive outlook on his work: optimistically recalling that the other job options in Takoradi are also not perfect. His story highlights some of the key tensions in the global gig economy. Workers try to make a living in a hyper-competitive planetary labour market; clients and platforms take zero responsibility for their working conditions; and yet workers are often relatively satisfied with that state of affairs because of the lack of other good options.

What will the book cover?

These short accounts do not tell the whole story of the gig economy, but they are an important starting point for understanding what is at stake. These two positions, one of a significant erosion of working conditions, the other of hard work, but new opportunities, capture the complex and sometimes contradictory nature of the phenomenon. The gig economy is full of other such stories: stories of hope, success, desperation, exploitation and everything in between. In this book, we draw on a combination of these accounts – from our own research as well as that of others – to tell the story of how digital technology is changing the nature of work. Our assumption is that workers' own experiences can be a powerful tool to explain broader changes in society (Woodcock, 2014a).

In chapter 1, we discuss where the gig economy came from. This starts by looking at other forms of work that came before it, exploring how precarious work has a much longer history, including on the docks and in factories. We then introduce the political economy, technological and social preconditions that have facilitated the rise of the gig economy. In chapter 2, we explore how the gig economy works by examining the platforms that organize this work. This involves first exploring how work platforms serve as intermediaries, then using Uber as an example to illustrate the key dynamics of this kind of operation. We explain the geographically tethered and cloudwork models. The focus shifts in chapter 3 as we move on to explore what it is like to work in the gig economy. This draws on the voices of workers, across both kinds of gig work. We present stories and experiences of workers we have met through our research, showing the complex relationship that workers have to this new kind of working arrangement. In chapter 4, we continue the focus on workers to outline how they are resisting and reshaping the gig economy, tracing emerging forms and trends. In the final chapter of the book, we summarize and reiterate the arguments we have made about the gig economy and platform work into four alternative futures, involving transparency, accountability, worker power and democratic ownership – as well as what *you* can do.

1

Where did the gig economy come from?

In this chapter, we critically examine how the gig economy came into being. We begin by considering earlier forms of work that were marked by on-demand labour and precarious conditions, and explore how these dynamics have shifted and transformed into what is commonly referred to today as 'gig work'. In other words, contingent jobs that happen through, via and on digital platforms.

In the early stages, new kinds of gigs held ambiguous possibilities. As Sarah Kessler (2018: x) recounts in a story from a startup founder, the gig economy had a promise that 'we could work for our neighbours, connect with as many projects as we needed to get by, and fit those gigs between band rehearsals, gardening, and other passion promises.' At this point, some commentators began talking about the 'sharing economy' (Sundararajan, 2017), a term that sounds very optimistic in light of the evidence that followed.

Although there have been changes in the gig economy, it still involves work. At its core, paid work involves a relationship in which one person sells their time to another. This entails transferring the ownership of labour power (the capacity to work) from the worker to the owner of capital (the owner of the things needed to produce work). As Marx (1976: 272) noted, this relationship requires workers who 'are free in a double sense'. They are free to choose who to work for, but at the same time (lacking capital) also 'free' from any other way of making a living other than by selling their labour power. This means that the worker is put at a disadvantage when selling their time. They rely on work to meet their needs, and are under constant pressure to both find and keep work. From this simple starting point of one person buying the time of another, work has developed into vastly more complex forms. Relationships of work now spread across the world, bound in complex chains of supply and demand, and bringing people together in new and different ways. However, despite the organizational complexities of modern work, the fundamental relationship between the person who buys time and the person who sells it remains a core concern.

Work has always been a changing phenomenon, both evolving over time and changing as it is fought over. The transformation of work has become a popular topic of research, debate and discussion. It is, after all, the activity that most of us will spend the majority of our time doing. The gig economy, particularly mediated through new digital platforms, is at the forefront of changes in work today. However, before focusing on the growth of the gig economy and its implications, we must consider how it is connected to the kinds of work that came before. The recent changes in work relationships are often discussed as a break from the so-called 'standard employment relationship'. This term refers to the kinds of work found in the Global North after the Second World War. For workers, this meant the expectation of a 'stable, socially protected, dependent, full-time job ... the basic conditions of which (working time, pay, social transfers) are regulated to a minimum level by collective agreement or by labour and/or social security law' (Bosch, 2004: 618–19). These kinds of work involved a 'link' between the work relationship (i.e. between the buyers and sellers of time) and the 'wider risk-sharing role of the welfare or social state', which came to prominence by the middle of the twentieth century (Fudge, 2017: 379). This meant that the risks of work were increasingly mitigated through social agreements, particularly with social security nets that could cushion workers from some negative outcomes, such as lack of work, poor working conditions or illness and accidents. Of course, referring to 'the standard employment relationship' carries with it the implication that this is somehow the 'normal' state of affairs. It then follows that precarious work should be understood as a break from this norm, as an attack that newly undermines long-standing conditions and benefits.

Precarious work, however, has a much longer history than the standard employment relationship. Work that is precarious (unstable or uncertain) is 'not necessarily new or novel to the current era; it has existed since the launch of paid employment as a primary source of sustenance' (Kalleberg, 2009: 2). As Bent (2017: 3) has argued, when looking at work over time and across the world, 'the relative stability and security of employment in the West post-WWII, then, was an anomaly.' And even within this context, it was reserved primarily for white men in the Global North. The standard employment relationship simply was not extended to many women and minorities, and certainly was not something seen extensively outside of a few industrialized economies. The standard employment relationship is therefore a bit of a misnomer, with unstable and precarious forms being both older and more widespread. The relationships of work are determined by the relative power of workers (selling their time) and capital (buying that time), along with the societal contexts in which work is carried out. It is therefore no surprise that what we think of as work is continuously evolving over time and space.

An important historical example of this kind of precarity is the dock work that took place in the East End of London, following the rapid growth of shipping docks in the nineteenth century that brought commodities from the colonies into the heart of imperial Britain. The raw cotton, sugar and tea could not get themselves out of the holds of the ships and into the warehouses, so large numbers of workers were needed. However, this did not mean employing people to work on the docks. It was estimated that 'about two-thirds of dock labour was casual', and as Weightman and Humphries (2007: 41) note, 'there was no guarantee of work from one week to the next and the vast majority of labourers were hired or fired on a day-to-day basis.' The arrival and departure of ships meant that dock work was not constant, with peaks in demand that needed to be met quickly. This was due to the strict timetables ships had to follow as they were caught up in a wider network of trade. Even before platforms, workers' schedules were shaped by global economic forces. Each day, prospective workers from London's deprived East End would queue up outside the gates of the docks, waiting to see if they would be 'called on' by a foreman. As Ben Tillett (1910: 8), a dock worker who later became a union organizer, explained:

> We are driven into a shed, iron-barred from end to end, outside of which a foreman or contractor walks up and down with the air of a dealer in a cattle market, picking and choosing from a crowd of men, who, in their eagerness to obtain employment, trample each other under foot, and where like beasts they fight for the chances of a day's work.

This is obviously a difficult environment for workers, who will be selling their time at a huge disadvantage. However, workers did not always passively accept this way of organizing work. In fact, it 'generated much anger among the dockers' (Tillett, 1910: 8). In the 1880s, other groups of workers were beginning to organize, most notably the 'Matchwomen' and their strike at the Bryant and May match factory in the East End of London (Raw, 2009). The strike was the result of low pay, long hours, fines, as well as severe health and safety problems related to the use of white phosphorous in the production process. After Annie Besant covered the conditions of the factory in a newspaper, the management of the factory tried to get the workers to sign a letter saying the claims were not true. After they refused, the managers tried to dismiss one of the workers. This triggered a strike of 1,400 women and girls. They elected their own committee to run the strike and successfully beat Bryant and May. As a result, they formed the largest female trade union. Louise Raw (2009: 224) argues that they were 'the mothers of the modern trade union movement'.

The success of the Matchwomen was then followed by the South

London Gas Workers strike in 1889. Then, in August of 1889, 100,000 dock workers went on strike over a reduction in 'plus' money – a bonus paid for unloading a ship quickly. The workers put forward a series of demands: wage increases, overtime pay, removing the 'plus' system, guarantees of minimum work and union recognition. The next month they won their strike demands. Their victory established strong, recognized trade unions on the dock, an important moment in the 'new unionism' movement in the UK (Duffy, 1961). Across different sectors, union membership rose from 750,000 members in 1888 to over 2 million by 1899. While the strikes did not end the precarious work on the docks, they proved that these workers could organize. This long period of struggle continued until the late 1960s, by which time 'virtually all dockers [were] on permanent terms' (Mankelow, 2017: 383). The London docks can therefore be seen as the 'ground on which the great battle against the most degrading forms of casualization was fought' (Mankelow, 2017: 384), and indeed – at least until the massive changes brought about by modernization and containerization in the late 1970s – dockers were able to win concessions from employers.

A similar story can be told of factory work. The development of factories entailed the movement of workers from the country-side to the city, with work concentrated within large workplaces like factories. Within the factory walls, 'employers could directly control when and how workers worked, adding new layers of insecurity to employment' (Bent, 2017: 4). In the early twentieth century in the US, for example, seasonal and peak demand pressures shaped the work relationship in many economic sectors. In the glass and textiles industries, workers would be employed for only three-quarters of the year to match demand, and broadly speaking, the numbers of jobs in industrial work could fluctuate by around 14 per cent, meaning many people risking loss of their employment. In the car industry, this fluctuation could be as high as 45 per cent (Jacoby, 2004: 16–17). However, by the end of the Second World War, in both the US and the Global North more broadly, these industrial jobs were highly unionized and workers had won much more stable employment conditions: protecting individual workers from down cycles, and placing more of the risk associated with doing business onto the firm rather than the individual worker.

There is a risk in seeing this development as a linear process – that is, one in which particular stages follow each other inevitably to a particular end. The thinking might go: first, industrialization introduces new forms of work, in which workers are made to accept unfair conditions. Next, industrial workers successfully organize and precarious conditions are overcome through the collective power of workers. However, because contemporary worker power is premised on the 'standard employment relationship' brought about by industrialization, all that workers have collectively achieved is threatened by waves of de-industrialization.

Although there are examples of the process developing like this, in many parts of the world the experience of industrialization was very different. For example, Bent (2017: 12) argues that large-scale industries were established in both Egypt and India under British imperial rule. This industrialization was deeply shaped by the exploitative relationships of the British Empire. Despite worker resistance, the industrialization that took place 'was highly disruptive to existing social and economic systems ... these changes resulted in the creation of working arrangements that were unstable, insecure, and contingent – in a word, precarious' (Bent, 2017: 14). However, as Webster et al. (2008) have argued, in low- and middle-income countries, the majority of workers were excluded from stable employment, unlike high-income countries. While there was a growth in more stable employment relations in low- and middle-income countries, the benefits of the standard employment contractor have never been widely felt by workers. Therefore, for most people, most of the time, work has been a precarious relationship. Precarity is the global norm.

The notion of precarious work is important for understanding the gig economy. A starting definition for precarious work can be found with the International Labour Organization (ILO, 2011: 5), which defines it thus:

In the most general sense, precarious work is a means for employers to shift risks and responsibilities on to workers. It is work performed in the formal and informal economy and is characterized by variable levels and degrees of objective (legal status) and subjective (feeling) characteristics of uncertainty and insecurity. Although a precarious job can have many faces, it is usually defined by uncertainty as to the duration of employment, multiple possible employers or a disguised or ambiguous employment relationship, a lack of access to social protection and benefits usually associated with employment, low pay, and substantial legal and practical obstacles to joining a trade union and bargaining collectively.

The problem, as Angela Mitropoulos (2005: 12) has noted, is that the term "'precariousness" is both unwieldy and indeterminate. If it is possible to say anything for certain about precariousness, it is that it teeters.' This is a useful starting point in 'emphasizing some of the tensions that shadow much of the discussion about precarious labour' (Mitropoulos, 2005: 12).

It is easy to observe the growth of this kind of precarious work, including temping, outsourcing, agency work and the gig economy. However, growth in the gig economy is not only driven by the private sector. In the UK, the largest employer of precarious workers is the state. There has been a huge growth of temporary workers across education, health and public administration, affecting both professionals and the lowest paid (McDowell et al., 2009: 9). The debate about precarious work is not just about whether or not there are workers with insecure contracts and conditions. However, the arguments about precarity really begin when the implications are considered. For Ulrich Beck (1992: 144), precarious work involved a break away from the system of either 'lifelong full-time work' or unemployment towards a 'risk-fraught system of flexible, pluralized, decentralized underemployment, which, however, will possibly no longer raise the problem of unemployment in the sense of being completely without a paid job'. In a similar vein, Pierre Bourdieu (1998: 95) argues that 'précarité' is a 'new mode of domination in public life ... based on the creation of a generalized and permanent state of insecurity aimed at forcing workers into submission, into the acceptance of exploitation'. Guy Standing (2011) goes even further, claiming that this has led to the formation of a new class: the 'precariat'.

What each of these positions is trying to argue is that there has been a significant break from the 'standard employment relationship', meaning we are now entering a new phase of the organization of work. The criticisms of these positions tend to focus on a rejection of two aspects – either the empirical basis or the implications of what is being argued. For example, Kevin Doogan (2009: 91) attempted to explain why there is a 'broad public perception of the end of jobs for life and the decline of stable employment' which operates alongside 'the rise in long-term employment'. At its core, his argument is an attempt to counter the ideology of neoliberalism by insisting that work is still really the same – and therefore trade unions can continue to organize in the same way that they have before. Similar critiques have been made against Guy Standing's assertion that an entirely new class of worker has been created. Perhaps the most useful of these comes from Richard Seymour (2012, quoted in Woodcock, 2017: 136), who argues that the concept of the precariat 'remains at best a purely negative, critical concept', unable to actually describe or explain a social class. Nevertheless, Seymour notes that it identifies something that requires further attention: if people feel more precarious, then this is an important dimension for understanding work.

Thinking about this in relation to the gig economy, it is self-evident that these new kinds of work are more precarious than established forms. Indeed, the gig economy operates in a context in which 'social, economic, and political forces have aligned to make work more precarious' (Kalleberg, 2009: 2). Kalleberg (2009: 6–8) discusses five factors that contribute to this. The first is a 'decline in attachment to employers', which can mean a greater number of different jobs held over a lifetime, along with a willingness to change jobs. The second is an 'increase in long-term unemployment', meaning more people are potentially seeking work. This is much sharper in low- and middle-income countries, particularly with large numbers of people who have never worked in 'standard' jobs. The third is 'growth in perceived job insecurity', which Seymour (2012, quoted in Woodcock, 2017: 136) identifies as meaning that regardless of whether or not work is actually becoming more precarious, people feel that it is, and it therefore has an effect. The fourth is 'a growth of non-standard work arrangements and contingent work', which we have already identified in the gig economy. The fifth is an 'increase in risk-shifting from employers to employees', a process that we also argue is taking place in the gig economy. This leaves us with the question of the implications of the growth of the gig economy, a topic we return to later in the book.

We have outlined this brief history of work to make the point that the precarious nature of work in the gig economy is not new. However, the gig economy represents a transformation and reorganization of work significant enough for us to be concerned about it. In the rest of this chapter, we argue that there are three key factors that have facilitated the growth of the gig economy. Firstly, broad political shifts taking place in the economy including worker power, state regulation and globalization and outsourcing. Secondly, the technological changes and new networks of connectivity that have allowed for the recruitment and management of geographically dispersed workers. And thirdly, social changes (including consumer attitudes and preferences, as well as gendered and racialized relationships of work) that have resulted in both employers and workers seeking more flexible working patterns.

The preconditions that shape the gig economy

There is a temptation to focus simply on technology as the motivating factor that brings the gig economy into being. However, there are a complex and interconnected set of preconditions that shape how the gig economy emerges in practice. In this section we discuss nine preconditions that shape the gig economy (see figure 1). Each of the preconditions are connected to the underlying factors of technology, society, political economy, or a combination thereof. We have placed the gig economy in the middle of the figure to indicate that each of these preconditions and factors shape the outcome. The rest of the chapter is structured around the nine preconditions: platform infrastructure (technology), digital legibility of work (technology), mass connectivity and cheap technology (technology and social), consumer attitudes and preferences (social), gendered and racialized relationships of work (social), desire for flexibility for/ from workers (social and political economy), state regulation (political economy), worker power (political economy), and globalization and outsourcing (political economy and technology). These preconditions certainly vary in importance between places and times, but we would argue that, together, they influence how most people think about today's gig economy. Although we use the term 'gig economy' in its singular form, we acknowledge that there are actually myriad *gig economies* all over the world that are experienced in significantly different ways. In other words, the experiences, practices and labour processes within gig economies are far from homogeneous. Nonetheless, speaking about *the* 'gig economy' allows us to draw out broad similarities amongst those practices and experiences.

Platform infrastructure

While we will return to the concept of 'platforms' in detail in chapter 2, it is worth noting how important platform infrastructure is as a precondition to the gig economy. The basic idea in the architectures of platforms that mediate work is to create a digital context in which buyers of labour power are able to connect with sellers of labour power (what economists call a 'two-sided market'). Uber's platform connects people who want a taxi ride with people who are willing to provide taxi rides. Fiverr's platform connects people looking for a graphic designer or video editor with people offering those services. Unlike older ways of connecting buyers and sellers of work, digital platforms make much of the process relatively seamless for both parties. On many platforms, it only takes a few minutes for a client seeking a service to issue a request through the platform, connect to a worker, and the worker to begin to perform that service. This use of the platform as the mechanism to connect clients and workers is what has led many

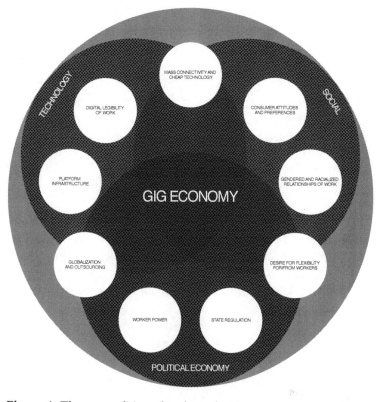

Figure 1 The preconditions that shape the gig economy
Design by Giorgio Marani

gig economy companies to attempt to claim that they themselves are not employers of the workers: that they simply provide a bridge between supply and demand. They claim, in other words, to be technology companies rather than taxi, delivery, home cleaning companies. Whilst this is certainly true, to some extent, for some platforms, the story is more complicated in other cases (a point we return to in more detail in chapter 2).

Current debates on the transformation of work often centre around technology, and imply that we are in uncharted territory due to the technological revolution that we find ourselves within. However, the idea that technology will change work is far from new. Take, for example, Marx's (1955 [1847]) often quoted line 'the handmill gives you society with the feudal lord; the steam-mill, society with the industrial capitalist.' The argument is not so much that the steam mill created the industrial capitalist, but rather that it would not have been possible to have an industrial capital-ist without the productive forces of the steam mill – the scale of production could not have supported this. Platform infrastructure operates in a similar way to the stream mill, providing the techni-cal basis for new organizations of work in the gig economy. The platform provides the ability for so-called technology companies to employ (or claim not to employ) large numbers of distributed workers.

Early platforms were set up around the turn of the millennium and were simply digital job boards that allowed workers to upload résumés or descriptions of their skills, and clients to upload infor-mation about the work that they needed done. Craigslist is perhaps the most well-known platform of this model. The architecture of the website influences the types of initial interactions that workers and clients can have with one another, but ultimately has little bearing on the labour process itself for most types of work.

Next came companies like Guru.com, vWorker and Elance, which allowed freelancers to upload profiles that highlighted their skills, leave feedback and bid for work. But it wasn't until the 2010s that platforms for geographically tethered work started becom-ing widely used. This was also not just a Western phenomenon. China's DiDi, India's Flipkart, and other copycats and genuine innovators developed infrastructures that could sit in between con-sumer demand and worker availability and skills.

What all platforms have in common is that they connect workers and clients who lack either proximity or synchronicity. In other words, they allow workers and clients to meet and transact who otherwise had no plans to be in the same place or share the same moments of co-presence. Today's platforms do this primarily through one of two mechanisms: negotiation-based matching and static-price matching. In the former system, clients and workers typically post information about their jobs and skills on a profile – allowing buyers to bid for workers and (more commonly) workers to bid for jobs. In the latter system, prices are fixed and no negotiation is possible. Uber and Deliveroo, for instance, don't allow drivers to negotiate their mileage rates. Fiverr conversely allows workers to set fixed prices for clients.

Uber's former CEO, Travis Kalanick, once noted[1] 'We are not setting the price. The market is setting the price ... We have algorithms to determine what that market is.' This selective framing conceals a lot of what platforms actually do. They are much more than just the matching infrastructure. Other core functions that they perform are facilitating payments, establishing trust mechanisms, surveillance of workers (and, in some cases, clients), and myriad sector-specific features like driver routing or panic buttons. The point here is that platforms are far from a simple marketplace in which clients and workers meet. They are designed with encoded features that impose rules and nudges onto all parties that they interact with. Platforms fundamentally shape the ways that gig work is carried out. But, as we will see, so too do many other factors.

Digital legibility of work

The ability to 'platformize' work – to use the platform infrastructure noted above – rests on an old problem of management: how to measure work. With the establishment of factories, workers were paid for their time in a workplace. This meant that managers wanted to ensure they got the most out of buying a worker's time. However, as most managers are not doing the work that workers do, it can be hard for them to understand whether workers are actually putting in enough effort. Not all workers want to work as efficiently as possible (especially when they are poorly paid or treated).

This deliberate slowing down of work – or 'soldiering' – became an obsession for Frederick Taylor (the 'father' of modern management theory). Taylor's solution was to meticulously record and measure the factory labour process. He argued that 'managers assume' the 'burden of gathering together all of the traditional knowledge which in the past has been possessed by the workmen and then the classifying, tabulating, and reducing this knowledge to rules, laws, and formulae' (Taylor, 1967: 36). This meant trying to make the work legible, making it visible so it could be understood by managers.

This managerial desire for legibility has developed with new forms of work. Factories became reorganized along Taylorist lines. Starting with time and motion studies, the factory floor would be investigated and measured in detail, calculating how much time each individual part of a task should take. The advent of the assembly line meant that production could then be sped up on this basis, trying to take control away from workers. Managers in call centres were able to use technological methods of surveillance to electronically measure the work process in great detail (Woodcock, 2017). Many work platforms follow on from these traditions, albeit without the physical supervision found in either factories or call centres. Some platform infrastructures allow the real-time location tracking and timing of every worker. This develops the forms of surveillance from the call centre, deploying them beyond the walls of a workplace (Woodcock, forthcoming). Some cloud platforms, in contrast, can monitor every digital activity performed by a worker on-platform.

The ability to organize work via a platform requires digital legibility. This means that some kinds of work are much more susceptible to this kind of 'routinization, reorganization, and rebundling' (Peck, 2017: 207). As we will discuss in this book, transportation, delivery and domestic work are proving comparatively easy to platformize. Similarly, forms of digital work that involve tasks that can be broken down and completed over the internet are, too. However, there are both forms of work and sites of work that are resistant to this kind of digital legibility.

It is worth thinking about labour in the gig economy as existing in a 'goldilocks zone' of legibility. Too little legibility and it becomes difficult to put work onto a platform in the first place. Here, layers of tacit rather than codified knowledge structure and govern the work process. Think of babysitters or security guards as jobs in which people tend to use personal recommendations, etc., that are hard to codify into platform ratings or databases. On the other hand, too much legibility and there is the risk that jobs become automated away. The Amazon dream of autonomous drones that can deliver parcels or the Uber dream of autonomous vehicles that can transport passengers are only possible in a world in which multiple overlapping spaces, activities and processes are highly digitally legible. Having a standardized addressing system, high-quality geospatial data, and the technology to produce and read those data has allowed large platforms to more effectively operate in some countries rather than others. For instance, a nascent delivery platform in Maputo, Mozambique, has to instead rely on a lot of human intervention and local knowledge to find delivery locations rather than automated geocoding to make their platform function.

Mass connectivity and cheap technology

Only a decade ago, the smartphone had just become popularized. Internet access was not something most people had in the palm of their hands, and most people used their phones for voice calls and SMS messages. Back then, internet penetration rates in many high-income countries were about 60–70 per cent – meaning that about a third of the population (and predominantly the poorest third of the population) in those countries had never used the internet. In most low-income countries, almost nobody was using the internet outside of elites, students and workers in a few select industries. For example, in 2006, the internet penetration rate in what the International Telecommunications Union (ITU) defined as 'developing countries' was 18 per cent.[2]

Much has changed since then! At the time of writing this book, over half of the world's population is now connected to the internet. So-called digital divides remain real, but in high-income countries almost everyone who wants to use the internet has at least some form of access. Penetration rates are lower in the rest of the world, with the ITU reporting that it is now 44.7 per cent for men and 37.5 per cent for women in the 'developing world'.[3] We are also in the midst of a 'mobile revolution' in many countries. The availability of cheap (<$20) smartphones and pay-as-you-go mobile plans have made the mobile phone an essential piece of technology to communities from Brazil to Burundi to Bangladesh. Urban regions of low- and middle-income countries are characterized by even higher levels of connectivity, and many of the working poor in cities as varied as Cairo, Bangkok, Nairobi and Rio all find ways of connecting.

As alluded to above, this connectivity for most people in low-, middle- and high-income countries is no longer confined to desktop machines plugged into a wall. A decade ago, internet access tended to be something limited to the home or the office, with many people still using dial-up modems. Today, the mobile phone is the device that most people use to connect. Instead of travelling to the internet, the internet now travels with many of us. The basic point here is that the world has very quickly become far more digitally networked than it used to be. Many of the populations of people who would be potential consumers and workers in the gig economy are no longer off the digital grid: they are integrated into the global network.

There are two primary ways in which this mass technologically mediated connectivity has been a key driver in moving work away from the traditional organizational structure of the firm and into the organizational forms of the contemporary gig economy. First, in their role as connectors, gig economy firms are now able to reach ever greater populations of clients and workers. This is especially important for the recruitment process (i.e. firms finding workers in the first place), but also for the day-to-day interactions that are a part of all gig economy labour processes. Drivers, delivery workers and data entry specialists are all continuously connected in order to carry out their jobs properly. Even though internet access is spreading rapidly across the world's population, many potential workers still only have access to 'feature phones' (i.e. pre-smartphones with no internet access). Some firms have therefore developed systems in which clients/consumers and workers require different technological affordances. In Maputo, Mozambique, for instance, there is a platform called Biscate that allows clients to request plumbers, builders, cleaners and other manual workers using a slick web-app, but the workers themselves receive requests through a more old-fashioned SMS system. The net effect is the same: that the world's workers are all being connected, and can potentially be enrolled into gig economy platforms.

Second, while most gig economy firms are focused on the provision of local services (for example, cleaning or food delivery), some gig economy firms have been able to set up global-scale platforms for services like data entry, graphic design or transcription that have fewer geographic limitations on where they need to be delivered from (see chapter 2 for more on this). These global platforms set up what you might think of as 'planetary labour markets' (Graham and Anwar, 2019). In the words of Guy Standing (2016), they enable a mass migration of labour, but not of people. Clients suddenly have a world of workers to choose from, and workers from around the global are placed into competition with one another – all made possible because the majority of humanity has now been connected to the global network.

Consumer attitudes and preferences

New economic activity requires consumer demand. An important precondition for the gig economy is therefore preferences and desires of end users and consumers. In some industries platforms have to encourage entirely new demands and behaviours. In others, they simply build on pre-platform practices. Delivery platforms, for instance, build upon a pre-existing consumer attitude of buying food remotely over the phone and having it delivered. The shift to digital platforms does not require a significant change in consumer attitudes, often being easier to do via an app than calling a landline phone number. The changes wrought by the gig economy therefore fit with Teresa Amabile's (1983) understanding of creativity: the formation of something that is both new and meaningful. The platformization of many of these activities is 'new', but they also have to be 'meaningful' in that they make sense to consumers and they are prepared to use them. There is a risk here in making assumptions about consumers' (as well as workers') digital literacy and ability to engage with these platforms.

Platform companies have thus far been relatively skilled in

harnessing consumer preferences in the face of bad press and threats of regulations. When Transport for London announced they would not renew Uber's operating licence upon its expiration on 30 October 2017, Uber launched a Change.org petition to fight this existential threat to their operations in London. They claimed there were 3.5 million 'Londoners who rely on Uber', and called on customers to sign the petition and share with '#SaveYourUber'. The petition was signed by 858,111 supporters.[4] This level of consumer and citizen activism can be frightening for any elected (or unelected) official trying to impose regulation. Platforms can frame regulators as being anti-innovation: arguing that they are dinosaurs taking away services that the populace need. The outcome of this sort of strategy is that regulators in most cities want to tread lightly and not unsettle sectors of the economy that provide jobs and satisfy consumer demands.

Conversely, though, consumer power can be turned against platforms. All large consumer-facing platforms are aware of the implications of bad press and, as a result, spend enormous sums on public relations and advertising. This is one of the few significant leverage points to improve platform work, and an issue we return to in more detail in the final chapter.

Gendered and racialized relationships of work

The gendered and racialized relationships of work that pre-exist the gig economy shape its outcomes, while also being reinforced and rearticulated in new ways. As Hunt and Samman (2019) have argued, 'on the whole it represents the continuation (and in some cases deepening) of long-standing structural, and gendered, inequalities.' Although many commentators will claim that 'machines don't discriminate', the issue is that people – and the people that design and build machines – do. And, it is people who use algorithms, databases, machines and platforms to engage with workers. Platforms, in other words, do not operate in some sort of alternate digital realm (Graham and Anwar, 2018). They are both produced by, and produce, the social – and thus gendered and racialized – ways in which we economically interact with one another.

The gendered relationships of work (that we will explore in detail later) can be seen in the inclusion and exclusion of women from different kinds of jobs in the gig economy. The roots of this can be traced to the gendering of work under capitalism more generally. For example, domestic work has always been a central component of capitalism. Factory labour would not have been sustainable without unpaid work in the home, caring for the current workers, while raising the children who would become future workers. Too often, this work has been seen as 'unproductive' in relation to the productive labour in a workplace, undermining its importance, along with devaluing the skills involved.

While the gendered basis of capitalism has not always involved such a straightforward distinction between women in the home and men at work, the creation of the household under capitalism has shaped domestic work in important ways. For example, as Mariarosa Dalla Costa and Selma James (1971: 10) have argued, 'where women are concerned, their labor appears to be a personal service outside of capital.' This can also entail the additional gendered burden of emotional labour at work (Hochschild, 1983), as well as the 'second shift' after work (Hochschild, 1989). For the housewife, this means the work is devalued, both in terms of remuneration and also with how it is valued as work. Dalla Costa and James (1971: 34) conclude that inside and outside of the home, women:

> have worked enough. We have chopped billions of tons of cotton, washed billions of dishes, scrubbed billions of floors, typed billions of words, wired billions of radio sets, washed billions of nappies, by hand and in machines.

Work within the household is still work. As Anderson (2000: 1) has argued, 'domestic work is vital and sustaining, and it is also demeaned and disregarded.' The pressures of unpaid domestic work increase the likelihood of women working in 'non-standard' jobs (Fredman, 2003). This means that women are much more likely to end up in segregated jobs, with a gender pay gap and fewer social protections throughout the life course, amongst other negative outcomes. Similarly, when it is 'paid domestic work in private households', it 'is disproportionately performed by racialized groups' (Anderson, 2000: 1).

The racialization of work has its roots in slavery, which played a key role in financing the industrial revolution. As Eric Williams (1994: 7) has argued, 'slavery was not born of racism: rather, racism was the consequence of slavery.' This is not to say that racism did not exist before slavery, but rather that the specific racialization of work emerged as a consequence of the exploitation of slave labour. Williams (1994) explores how economic forces led to and then replaced slavery, rather than humanitarian concerns. Racism continues to deeply shape the experiences of work. For many workers, this is linked to migration status – and those without legal migration status are particularly at risk (Ryan, 2005). Migrants, for example, are 'often forced to accept the most precarious contracts, in jobs incommensurate with their skill levels' (McDowell et al., 2009: 4).

The majority of precarious workers are non-unionized and 'have been marginalized' (Pollert and Charlwood, 2009: 357), whether through gender, race or migration status. Therefore, those workers who find themselves in low paid 'non-standard' work are often not covered by any of the 'three regulatory regimes – collective bargaining, employment protection rights, and the national insurance system' (Fredman, 2003: 308). For example, migrant cleaners across London are often not covered by any of these regulatory regimes (Woodcock, 2014b). In the case of migrant cleaners, the gendered and racialized relationships combine to create a deeply exploitative workplace. More broadly, these relationships shape what kinds of work are available to a prospective worker, their likelihood of getting a job, along with their experiences of working it.

Desire for flexibility for/from workers

The next social precondition is also connected to political economy. It is a desire for flexibility that has come from both employers and workers, with the shifts in cultures and social practices that make flexibility desirable for both. This is not to argue that the structural changes we have discussed in the first set of preconditions are not important. Clearly, the changes within the broader economy are driving a restructuring of work, whether ostensibly as 'flexicurity' (European Commission, 2008) or more explicitly as a project to dismantle previous protections or benefits at work. However, this removes any sense of agency from workers themselves. Workers are not passive actors at work. While most workers might be free from any other way to meet their needs than through work, they are still (relatively) free to choose between different kinds of available work.

As both of us have found in our research, many workers in the gig economy are keen to stress that they appreciate the flexible aspects of the work, even if they then have other grievances. For example, a worker at Deliveroo explained that they preferred it as:

> you're not selling anything, you're not selling yourself so there's no emotional labour in it and I think that's why it's been like a job that I've stuck at longer than other shit jobs because I find it a lot easier to not do that sort of selling yourself side of things.

The alternative kinds of work that they described included service work based in a restaurant or working the phones in a call centre. This, despite the fact they still described Deliveroo as a 'shit job', made it comparatively better than the conditions in high-pressure call centres (Woodcock, 2017). Similarly, another worker explained that they 'wanted to work outside and with a bicycle, because it's my passion working with a bicycle'. For younger workers, the gig economy offers the potential – and it is important to stress that this is a potential, as we discuss further later in the book – for different ways of working. This is particularly important considering the rise of what David Graeber (2018) has called 'bullshit jobs', forms of work that appear to be meaningless busywork. The desire to escape from these kinds of jobs provides a ready supply of labour power to be put to work in new ways.

In low- and middle-income countries, even relatively high-skilled workers have tended to be quite constrained by the boundaries of their local labour markets. With most cities in the

Global South characterized by high unemployment rates and a lack of opportunities, it is not surprising that many workers in those places have jumped at the chance to find jobs in the gig economy. Furthermore, because the closed employment relations that have been the norm in much of the Global North were never that common in the South, the open employment relationships of the gig economy tend to be perceived less negatively by southern workers (Wood et al., 2019b).

It is also worth noting that gig economy employers are clearly pushing for ever more flexible forms of work. In many cases, employers refuse to even acknowledge their own role in the employment relationship. Uber and Deliveroo frame themselves as technology companies rather than taxi operators or delivery companies, respectively. Their drivers are referred to as 'partners', not workers, and certainly not employees. Constructing the relationship in this way has involved the widespread use of a different kind of relationship, far removed from the 'standard employment relationship'. Instead of an employment relationship, many kinds of gig work instead use versions of self-employment and independent contractor status. This goes further than the removal of stable employment that we have traced since the 1970s, representing a breaking of the employment relationship and the freeing of platforms from many of the responsibilities and requirements that used to be involved.

This feeling, or subjectivity, is also a key part of the debate on precarious work. For example, Mitropoulos (2005: 13) has argued that the 'flight from "standard hours" was not precipitated by employers but rather by workers seeking less time at work' and connects it to what 'the Italian Workerists dubbed the "refusal of work" in the late 1970s'.[5] Rather than seeing workers as passive recipients of the structural changes in work, the concept is part of politicizing work. As part of this, Anthony Iles (2005: 36) warns of the risks of considering struggles at work today only 'in terms of battles for better legislation'. The risk of only seeking to return to older forms of work 'misses the opportunity to investigate the tendency for self-organized (or "disorganized") labour to develop a more generalized struggle'. From this perspective, precarity becomes part of a political 'project to dismantle the mass worker as the central object for labour struggles and place it on the shoulders of the more encompassing but diffuse idea of the precarious worker' (McKarthy, 2005: 55). Here, too, attention is drawn to the heterogeneity of precarious workers, taking into account two kinds of precarious workers: 'BrainWorkers' who have specialist skills and relative bargaining power, and 'ChainWorkers' in the service industry and 'the only thing they have to sell is their labour' (McKarthy, 2005: 57). Meanwhile, gig economy employers find ever more ways to divide up the work process so that workers can always be called upon in an on-demand way.

State regulation

In order to address the issue state of regulation, we need to start by making sense of 'neoliberalism'. However, the problem with using this term is that, as Jamie Peck (2013: 133) explains, it is a 'rascal concept'. While it is often used 'with pejorative intent' to refer to a wide range of economic problems, usually that is the end of the argument – as if without neoliberalism, everything would be fine. However, an important starting point for understanding neoliberalism is David Harvey's (2007: 2) argument, that it is 'in the first instance a theory of political economic practices that propose that human well-being can best be advanced by liberating individual entrepreneurial freedoms and skills within an institutional framework characterized by strong private property rights, free markets, and free trade'. However, as we shall discuss, the way in which this is put into practice is more complicated. Therefore, as Peck (2013: 153) notes, using the term 'must not be a substitute for explanation; it should be an occasion for explanation'. In order to explain how neoliberalism has facilitated the growth of the gig economy, there are two turning points to begin from.

The first is the economic crisis of the 1970s and the response, particularly in the UK and US in the late 1970s and 1980s. This 'structural crisis' saw the end of the economic growth of the post-war period (Duménil and Lévy, 2005: 9). The high-point of the 'standard employment relationship' discussed in the previous section was also now under serious threat as unemployment and inflation grew. In this turning point, as with the next, the crisis provided the opportunity for sweeping reforms, part of the 'shock doctrine' (Klein, 2008) of neoliberalism. In the UK, Prime Minister Margaret Thatcher dealt a serious blow to the trade union movement by defeating the miners' strike (one of the world's largest ever strikes that resulted in defeat for the workers). In the US, Ronald Reagan defeated the air traffic control workers. For both, this was followed with a programme of reforms that has come to characterize neoliberalism: attacking workers' terms and conditions, the rolling back of the welfare state and sectoral subsidies, and increasing privatization and use of market forces (Harvey, 2007: 12). In the UK, this also entailed tax reduction and significant deregulation, both financial but also relating to work (Woodcock, 2018a). As Thompson and Ackroyd (1995: 618) have summarized, from 1979 in the UK:

> Political action by a succession of Conservative administrations has also clearly shaped the broader landscape. Three significant dimensions of policy can be identified: a strategy of de-regulation of labour markets and promotion of a low wage, low skill economy as a means of attracting inward investment; competitive tendering and internal markets in the public sector; and the sustained legislative assault on union organisation, employment rights and collective bargaining.

This long period of change has shaped the current state of the employment relationship. In particular, the growth of the service industries since the 1970s has seen another phase in which workers have to sell their labour power without much ability to collectively bargain over the terms. At the same time, the labour market was '"deregulated" and labour made more "flexible"', as part of a political project to undermine workers' rights, restoring 'management's "right to manage"' (Munke, 2005: 63). A key part of this has been 'a general move away from the full employment goal towards activation policies' (MacGregor, 2005: 144). The result has been a growth in underemployment, and a decline of stable employment. It has also involved an increasing polarization of the types of jobs available (Kaplanis, 2007), with a growth in the number of low-paid 'lousy jobs' at the bottom (Goos & Manning, 2007).

If the first turning point put neoliberalism into practice, the second forced more action. The 2008 financial crisis, precipitated by a crisis of subprime mortgages, had its roots in the crisis of profitability that remained unresolved from the 1970s. As Peck (2013: 134) has noted, 'after doubling up' in the previous period, 'neoliberalism has doubled down' since 2008. The response from the European Commission (2008) was to focus on the labour market aspects of the crisis, stressing that 'EU member states should develop measures within a policy framework informed by the principles of "flexicurity"' (Heyes, 2011: 643). However, the reality was not a combination of flexibility and security, but rather the 'dominant trend has been towards less security' (Heyes, 2011: 643).

Since 2008 there have been many claims about an economic upturn or the beginnings of hopeful economic growth. However, as Paul Mason (2016) has argued, the years following have been a jobless recovery. Rather than the creation of new jobs and the sharing of the benefits of economic growth, there has been an increase in low-paid and insecure work. This has been facilitated by the rolling back of employment protections. There have also been aggressive changes to the welfare state including labour market activation policies that are forcing workers into low-paid work, often subsidized by the state. Alongside these policies, some countries are actively encouraging the gig economy as a potential source of economic prosperity and progress. South Korea, for instance, is investing public money in platforms in the hope that they will ultimately contribute to economic growth.[6] Kenya, likewise, is rushing to sign up people to its Ajira Digital programme: a scheme that intends to turn up to a million young Kenyans into platform workers as a way of tackling the youth unemployment crisis in the country.

The gig economy, particularly in the case of 'lean platforms', is successfully taking advantage of this context, which 'ultimately appears as an outlet for surplus capital in an era of ultra-low interest rates and dire investment opportunities rather than the vanguard destined to revive capitalism' (Srnicek, 2017: 91). The glut of money made by companies in the technology industry is increasingly being held outside of the home country of the firm, not brought back for fear of taxation and without anywhere profitable to invest. This is a continuation of the crisis of profitability referred to before, but under increased pressure as there is a vast amount of money needing to be spent on something. In essence, those with large amounts of capital were finding that their money was not growing in traditional bank savings or investments, and so they looked for avenues to invest. The fledgling gig economy became the perfect outlet for this through the growth of venture capital. In this way, the development of technology then feeds back into the gig economy as investment, as well as providing the tools upon which it is being built.

Worker power

This neoliberal context has greatly weakened employment protections, along with facilitating the growth of a pool of potential workers who are struggling to meet their needs through existing work opportunities. The changes in production identified by Ricardo Antunes (2012: 37) have had a significant impact on work:

> extensive deregulation of labour-rights, eliminated on a daily basis in all corners of the world that have industrial production and services; increase in the fragmentation of the working class, precarisation and subcontracting of the human force that labours; and destruction of class-unionism and its transformation into docile unionism, based on partnership.

The failure of the trade union movement to fully adapt to deindustrialization has also greatly reduced the collective power of workers relative to capital. In these contexts, trade unions 'face considerable obstacles to extending their presence in private services, not least from hostile employers' (Williams and Adam-Smith, 2009). In many contexts, as workers' power is reduced, and the deregulated environment allows for new kinds of employment relationships. Significant risks are shifted from employers to workers, while at the same time making workers bargain as individuals rather than as collectives. In this way, Ravenelle (2019: 6) argues that 'despite its focus on emerging technology', the gig economy 'is truly a movement forward to the past' in terms of conditions and protections at work.

These changes have limited the capacities for workers to shape their own work. In many contexts, workers have not operated within the institutional framework of trade unions that were integrated, at least in part, into capitalism in high-income countries. However, the decline of traditional trade unionism does not mean that workers do not resist, rather that the resistance is not expressed in forms that have been used previously. This does mean that many workers miss the protection of institutional forms of worker power. In most of the gig economy – despite some exceptions that we will discuss later in the book – there are no active trade unions. This means that management are more likely to act unilaterally, without the checks of collective bargaining or negotiation.

Globalization and outsourcing

The final precondition that has deeply shaped the gig economy in its current form is a combination of political economy and technology: the effects of globalization and outsourcing. This is a development and intensification of the outsourcing of call centres from high-income countries to low- and middle-income countries, for example, from the UK to India (Taylor and Bain, 2005). This laid the organizational basis for wider business process outsourcing that has become today's online outsourcing. However, globalization has not only meant the shifting of work and trade to different parts of the world, but also brought about a generalization of what Barbrook and Cameron (1996) have termed the 'Californian Ideology', referring to the encouragement of deregulated markets and powerful transnational corporations. While this is often linked to the rise of 'cognitive capitalism' (Moulier-Boutang, 2012) and the companies creating the software and platforms in Silicon Valley, it increasingly becomes a driver to open up markets in low- and middle-income countries too.

Alongside this ideological globalization, there has been a spread of common or shared technological infrastructures. For example, the IP addressing system, Visa/Mastercard/Amex (as well as new mobile) payment platforms, the GPS system, Google Maps as a base layer, and the Apple and Google Android phone operating systems, allow an increased internationalization of working practices. This globalization of technology has allowed platform companies to build their services on top of this globalized stack of infrastructures and scale relatively quickly. In some cases (such as platforms that rely heavily on GPS), it is also noteworthy that platforms are built on infrastructures that were made possible by early state investments. Firms can use these global infrastructures and standards to quickly scale up or down in response to changing market conditions, and quickly adapt existing models to new contexts.

The rise of the gig economy

This chapter has shown that the gig economy is characterized by not just firms using platforms to create two-sided marketplaces that connect buyers and sellers and services. It is also not just an extension of previous forms of labour market precarity. There is something new here. The gig economy is the combination of the nine factors which create an organizational form in which firms have an on-demand workforce that differs from previous types of precarious jobs. Dock workers could not be hired in intervals measured in minutes; they were still bound into local labour markets, needing to unload boats in particular places. The gig economy changes all of that with new controls over the temporality of work. Workers have the freedom to choose when they would like to work, but the other side of that bargain means that precarity exists at a much finer scale than ever before (down to the minute), and competition is expanded to a scale never before seen. This involves the expansion of the spatial scales of competition and the contraction of the temporal scales of the responsibility of the firm for its workers. This is outsourcing reconfigured for the new economy.

We should note that it is notoriously difficult to measure the size of the gig economy. There are two issues at play here: the data that are available, and how you define the gig economy in the first place. There have been claims that, in the US, contingent work and independent contracting is actually less common today than it was in the early 2000s.[7] Those claims have then been used to extrapolate that the gig economy is a shrinking phenomenon. In this book we take a narrower definition of the gig economy. We use the term not as a reference to all 'non-standard' employment; but rather in a way that is more in line with how it is deployed in everyday speech. In other words, as a reference to independent contracting that happens through, via and on digital platforms.

Using that narrower framing, reliable statistics on either the size of the market or the number of workers is extremely difficult to ascertain. In one of the few attempts to construct a headcount of gig workers, Richard Heeks (2017) estimates that up to seventy million people are registered on online outsourcing platforms. However, only about 10 per cent are likely to be active at any given time. Workers are also able to create accounts on multiple platforms: a fact that further inflates those estimates.

Data that capture more of the breadth of gig economy activities can be found in a survey conducted by Herman et al. (2019). The authors surveyed people in seven African countries, and found that 1.3 per cent of adults in those countries earned income from a platform. Using a very different estimation model, Heeks (2017) came up with a remarkably similar statistic. He estimates that there are between 30 and 40 million platform workers in the Global South (40 million would represent 1.5 per cent of the Global South workforce). In the Global North, there are huge variances in measurements and estimations of the number of platform workers (OECD, 2019). A McKinsey study of 8,000 workers in France, Germany, Spain, Sweden, the UK and the US found that 1.5 per cent of respondents had earned income from platforms (Manyika et al., 2016). A study by Huws et al. (2016) in seven European countries found much larger numbers. Their findings ranged from a low end of 9 per cent of the working population who had earned income from work platforms in the UK – slightly lower than the findings of Huws and Joyce (2016) discussed earlier – to 19 per cent in Austria. Eurobarometer similarly found that platform workers comprised less than 1 per cent of the population (in Malta) to 11 per cent (in France).

Ultimately, the reality is that all of these statistics are very rough numbers. But, however we slice the numbers, we do know that there are a lot of platform workers out there – probably tens of millions of them. And we also know that just a few years ago there were orders of magnitude fewer. Ever more work, in other words, is being mediated by platforms. Ever more work is entering the gig economy. We are in the midst of a profound period of economic experimentation into ways of organizing work that move beyond the traditional employment contract; ways of organizing work to be piecemeal, contingent and fragmented.

However, what we are not arguing is that gig work is the only kind of work that we should be concerned with. We have sympathy with Moody's (2017: 69) warning that focusing solely on this can 'trivialize the deeper reality of capitalism, its dynamics, and the altered state of working-class life' (Moody, 2017: 69). Gig work has to become numerically dominant to have far-reaching effects. As Callum Cant (2019) argues in his book on Deliveroo, the gig economy operates as a capitalist laboratory through which new techniques of management, control, worker exploitation and the extraction of profit are tested and refined. The success of these experiments, then, has much wider implications over the longer term as they are applied to other kinds of work.

There are now attempts the world over to introduce the gig economy model into almost every conceivable sector; to create the next Uber for X. As platforms expand into ever more sectors of the economy, we do not yet know which jobs will and will not become Uberized. However, by analysing what preconditions bring the gig economy into being, how the gig economy works, and who it works for, we can get a sense of how the gig economy might look in years to come and what effects might be introduced into other work. It is into this laboratory of the gig economy that we now turn.

2

How does the gig economy work?

This chapter is about how gig economy platforms operate. It takes examples from two fundamentally different types of gig work – *geographically tethered work* and *cloudwork*, to illustrate how they operate in practice (see figure 2). Through case studies of existing platforms, we explain the actual operation of the gig economy, focusing on how the work is organized, the practices of companies, how money is made, and we map the scale and spread of the phenomenon, to provide an overall picture of the gig economy worldwide. By examining business models and management practices that are either currently in use or in development, the chapter provides a combined view from the perspectives of the platform, the client and the employer. It therefore seeks to understand the motivations for the world of work they are each instrumental in creating. The ways in which platforms make a profit and organize their value chains have important implications for the experiences that follow in chapter 3.

What is a platform?

While the gig economy – or at least the prevalence of 'gigs' and precarious work – is not exactly new, platforms do represent a significant break with the past. As Nick Srnicek (2017: 6) has argued, the platform economy needs to be understood as a response to the economic crisis of the 1970s and the 'long decline in manufacturing profitability', which after 2008 saw the platform emerge 'as a new business model, capable of extracting and controlling immense amounts of data'. This connects platform infrastructure with other political economy preconditions discussed previously.

The designation 'platform' comes from its more traditional usage as a raised surface on which people can stand. In this context, the platform is a digital environment upon which other software can be run. In organizational terms, Nick Srnicek (2017: 48) argues that:

> Platforms, in sum, are a new type of firm; they are characterized by providing the infrastructure to intermediate between different user groups, by displaying monopoly tendencies driven by network effects, by employing cross-subsidization to draw in different user groups, and by having a designed core architecture that governs the interaction possibilities.

For the gig economy, as we have written elsewhere, 'the common feature of all digital labour platforms is that they offer tools to bring together the supply of, and demand for, labour' (Graham and Woodcock, 2018: 242). Similarly, Niels van Doorn (2017: 901) describes these organizations as 'platform labour intermediaries that, despite their self-presentation as tech companies, operate as new players in a dynamic temporary staffing industry.'

The platform therefore operates as a kind of intermediary for work. However, this intermediate function operates with a spectrum of control. For example, in figure 2, platform work is compared to traditional waged employment. In this case, there are (usually) high levels of temporality (workers are engaged for longer job durations) and the work has high levels of geographic stickiness (the work needs to be completed in a specific place). At the opposite end is cloudwork (microwork), in which there are very low levels of temporality and geographic stickiness: the jobs are of very short duration and can be completed from anywhere with an internet connection. As with online freelancing, which exhibits slightly more geographical stickiness, as well as the potential for longer job duration, platforms provide a way for a client to connect with a worker and set their own rates and conditions, following the model of Upwork or Amazon Mechanical Turk. The platform hosts the requests for work and the response of prospective workers. Geographically tethered platform work requires workers to be in a particular place. This means the platform exerts more control, often involving many of the same controls that a traditional waged employer would deploy.

Across both cloudwork types and geographically tethered work, platforms present themselves as different to traditional waged employment. At the core of the gig economy is a controversy over the classification of the people involved. In most countries, work can be categorized as conducted by an employee or someone who is self-employed. Self-employment means that a person runs their own business and therefore takes responsibility for its successes

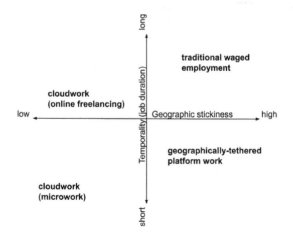

Figure 2 The spatiality and temporality of platform work

or failures, while also not having the rights or responsibilities of employees.[1] The issue at stake here is that being classified as self-employed means losing employment rights – although the protections that these afford can vary widely around the world. In most countries where there are binary employment statuses, this also makes it challenging to consider how gig workers fit within the traditional employee categorization.[2]

Platforms the world over prefer to use the self-employment classification as this allows them to contract work out to workers without meeting many employment regulations. It also means that workers have no access to rights around unfair dismissal or the right to organize in a trade union, issues that we will return to later. It is worth stating that we have not written this book as lawyers, and it is not our intent to get mired in debates about who is and is not an employee versus an independent contractor. We rather take the position that anyone exchanging labour power for money is a worker irrespective of their actual categorization. And that every worker deserves a set of minimum rights and protections. That said, it seems clear that many workers in the gig economy are misclassified as self-employed: a strategy that clearly offers more benefits to platforms than it does to workers. In the case of Uber, for example, this was supported by the employment judge in the workers' rights tribunal who stated: 'The notion that Uber in London is a mosaic of 30,000 small businesses linked by a common "platform" is, to our minds, faintly ridiculous.'[3]

This contractual outsourcing represents an evolution of a much older trend towards outsourcing. The trend towards outsourcing began in the 1970s as part of a push for lower costs and higher profits. It involved an organization taking parts of their operations like facility maintenance, cleaning or customer services and tendering them out to external companies. In the Global North, outsourcing became prevalent in both the private and public sector, driving down costs to either increase profits or meet internal targets. For example, in the UK it has become common for universities to outsource cleaning to private companies. This means a section of previously directly employed staff become employed by a private company. This creates a twofold advantage for university management. First, the responsibility for those workers (including how much workers are paid and their working conditions) is taken on by an external organization; second, by tendering out the contracts to the lowest bidder the university can drive down costs. Platforms have been able to take this project of outsourcing to a new level. What Srnicek (2017: 49) describes as 'lean platforms', are those 'which attempt to reduce their ownership of assets to a minimum and to profit by reducing costs as much as possible'. This was summarized by Tom Goodwin (2015) who noted that 'Uber, the world's largest taxi company, owns no vehicles. Facebook, the world's most popular media owner, creates no content.'

Despite the lean nature of these platforms, real people are still needed to drive cars for Uber, while Facebook needs people to serve as both content producers and moderators. The expensive capital costs are outsourced, retaining only the barest minimum of staff. This also extends to infrastructure costs, with many platforms running on Amazon web servers, renting the capacity needed. As Goodwin (2015) continues, 'the interface is where the profit is'. The elements that are retained by the company are the interface: methods to extract, analyse and use data. These aspects are not outsourced to any other company. Instead, the data are hoarded and put to work. Thus, the platform is like a shell, with just the 'bare extractive minimum – control over the platform that enables a monopoly rent to be gained' (Srnicek, 2017: 76).

The organization of the platform means that they are particularly reliant on network effects. The more workers and users on the platform, the greater the benefits of participating (Srnicek, 2017: 45). Conversely, if there is significant competition between platforms in any particular sector, those network effects are diminished. For instance, multiple taxi apps in a city will fragment both the driver and customer base, increasing waiting times and reducing the ease of access. Many platforms have been able to achieve these network effects relatively easily because of their relatively rapid expansion. In the case of Uber, there is no need for the platform itself to buy new cars. Instead, expansion is limited by server capacity, effective advertising and available workers. These two aspects combine to 'mean that platforms can grow very big very quickly' (Srnicek, 2017: 46).

The quick growth has meant that platforms have sprung up across different kinds of work. For the worker, this does not necessarily mean that their work process has substantially changed. A traditional minicab or taxi driver who becomes an Uber driver is still driving customers around, while a care worker moving onto Care.com is still providing care. However, a point that we will return to throughout the book is that this experience is differentiated between the Global North and the Global South. Some workers are moving from relatively formalized jobs onto platforms, whilst for others who have only ever worked in the informal sector, platform work is relatively formalized.

The case of Uber

The most recognizable geographically tethered platform is without doubt Uber. The platform has 3.9 million drivers across the world.[4] It holds so much brand recognition that the company is regularly used as a synonym for new platform ideas: the 'Uber for X' (Srnicek, 2017: 37), or even becoming a verb: to Uberize, meaning 'to change the market for a service by introducing a different way of buying or using it, especially using mobile technology'.[5] At its core, Uber provides something quite straightforward. The idea of transporting people as a job (i.e. taxis) has been around for centuries – albeit in a variety of forms such as drivers with horse-drawn carriages. Transporting customers for a fee has since been transformed through technology and licensing – moving from taxi-ranks and customers flagging them down in the street, to centralized controllers with radios, and medallion systems to limit driver numbers. What Uber provides is an app that connects drivers and passengers, in a straightforward exchange of money for transportation. It has neither invented the role of the driver, nor the need of the passenger, but rather a new way to connect them.

It is now possible to use the same app to quickly and reliably order an Uber in more than 600 cities around the world. Indeed, if Uber did not offer a genuine benefit to consumers, it would not have grown at such a rapid rate. This bringing together of workers and customers on geographically tethered platforms requires the building of trust by platforms. After all, the prospect of a stranger driving you around is a tough sell. Unlike pre-platform offerings, there is no obvious office or representative to complain to. Platforms instead rely on building consumer trust through rating systems and other forms of tracking.

Taking the example of London, the city has long had a two-tiered taxi arrangement. First, the famous black cabs, with drivers who learn 'the knowledge' of London streets.[6] These are taxis that can be flagged down on the street without prior booking. This is different to the second kind, minicabs, which had to be arranged by phone. These needed different kinds of operator licences to black cabs, along with no need to do 'the knowledge'. Minicabs had a reputation for unreliability, with the dispatcher often promising a cab was 'on the way' without any way for the customer to verify that it actually was. What Uber has been able to do is provide a customer interface that is appealing to smartphone users. No longer waiting on the phone to order a cab, but a slick designed app that orders the Uber car to the customer's location, showing not only the time until arrival, but also details on the driver and number-plate. This means no longer needing phone numbers for different local taxi companies, and no need for the customer to explain where they are. What Uber has achieved is a new way to intermediate a long-standing relationship between driver and passenger – something that has also involved huge amounts spent on advertising and branding.

Uber's initial offering was a high-end service. However, its main success has been UberX, a low-cost offering. In the US, the UberX version relies on 'unlicensed drivers with their own cars, many without commercial insurance' (Slee, 2015: 57). However, in the UK (as well as many other countries), Uber drivers have to have a private hire licence. In addition to UberX, the company has experimented with luxury services like Uber Black, pooling customers in the same car, as well as deliveries. This has been funded by astonishingly large tranches of venture capital funding, with $24.2 billion so far.[7] That funding has facilitated the rapid growth of the company, through its ability to run at a loss while spending venture capital money accrued through investment. From the start Uber provided special offers, bonuses and incentives to build the network effects needed to sustain its model. At first, a city with only a few Uber drivers could not sustain an Uber service for long, like a telephone network with few telephones. However, once 'it becomes established, Uber takes a bigger slice of each dollar and often cuts fares. Over time, Uber has taken a larger and larger slice of every fare' (Slee, 2015: 65). This is how Uber makes money with the platform: by taking a commission from every journey that a driver makes.

The success of Uber is also partly explained by its engagement with regulation and transport policy. As Travis Kalanick (2013) – the former CEO of Uber – explained:

> In most cities across the [US], regulators have chosen not to enforce against non-licensed transportation providers using ridesharing apps. This course of non-action resulted in massive regulatory ambiguity leading to one-sided competition which Uber has not engaged in to its own disadvantage.

This coyly phrased lack of 'disadvantage' has actually proven to be incredibly advantageous for Uber. As Trebor Scholz (2017a: 44) emphasizes: 'Uber is a labor company, not simply a tech startup, which means that it is reliant on the availability of an abundance of cheap labor and a permissive regulatory environment.' Despite its reliance on labour, Uber's business model involves avoiding sales taxes, the cost of vehicles, repairs, insurance, and meeting obligations for social security for its drivers. The main legislative loophole that Uber has taken advantage of is the categorization of its workers as self-employed independent contractors. In the process, 'Uber created a fundamental cultural shift in what it means to be employed' (Rosenblat, 2018: 4).

However, Uber has gone way beyond just taking advantage of lack of effective regulation, through its concerted public relations and lobbying campaigns. The company employs and is advised by political operatives such as Jim Messina (the former White House

Deputy Chief of Staff) and David Plouffe (Barack Obama's 2008 campaign manager). Pollman and Barry (2016) refer to this sort of strategy as 'regulatory entrepreneurship' – 'pursuing a line of business in which changing the law is a significant part of the business plan'. Kalanick has described the rise of the company as analogous to a political campaign in which 'the candidate is Uber and the incumbent is an asshole called "taxi"' (Kalanick and Swisher, 2014). Another documented tactic is the use of 'greyballing' to evade regulation. This involves the 'greyball' tool developed by Uber, which take the data collected by the app through its normal operation in order to 'identify and circumvent officials who were trying to clamp down on the ride-hailing service'.[8] The use of the tool was approved by Uber's legal team and has been running since at least 2014. For example, in Portland, Oregon, Uber was operating without approval. Uber gathered the details of city officials and 'greyballed' them, providing 'a fake version of the app, populated with ghost cars, to evade capture', including cancelling any rides they were able to hail. Uber justified this as part of its 'violation of terms of service' (VTOS) programme, aiming to prevent anyone misusing the service from accessing it. However, it has also widely been seen as a method for deliberately evading regulation by preventing officials from finding out whether Uber was operating within their jurisdiction.

The 'independent contractor' status frees Uber from many obligations to its drivers. Of particular importance are pay and rights to collective bargaining, which we discuss in chapter 4 and the Conclusion. Among the many concerns raised about the Uber platform is how much money its workers make. Uber's marketing campaign has worked hard to assuage fears, claiming at one point that Uber drivers in New York City earn over $90,000 a year (without giving a sense of the costs required to make this amount). However, as Trebor Scholz (2017a: 43) has noted 'nobody was able to verify' this claim, leading him to conclude that 'Uber's marketing campaign is falsifying the facts'. In an investor meeting, Uber's former CFO Brent Callinicos stated that it could easily raise rates to between 25 and 30 per cent. Mike Novogratz, a venture capitalist who was present at the meeting, asked a question: 'You've got happy employees, you've got happy customers, you've got happy shareholders. The holy triumvirate are all really excited about your company. Why are you going to risk that and push the employees' salary down 5%?' As reported in SF Gate, Callinicos simply responded 'because we can'.[9] As Slee (2015: 65) has noted, the experiment with taking 30 per cent actually means that Uber takes a bigger cut than most medallion owners.[10] What this also shows is a unilateral management attitude on platforms, particularly as they engage self-employed independent contractors.

Of course, the challenge of estimating how much drivers are paid is only difficult for those of us outside the platform. Within the platform, huge amounts of data are collected about the drivers and journeys. Uber knows where its drivers are, where they have been, the routes they have taken, the cost of each journey, and how it was rated by the passenger. Part of this hunger for data can be explained by Uber's ambition to introduce self-driving cars.[11,12] The huge quantities of data provide a training set that can be used to train artificial intelligence self-driving, meaning that the losses made in the short term could be offset by the potential for longer-term gains if Uber has the majority on self-driving vehicles.[13] Anyone in doubt about the granularity of Uber's data collection should note the so-called 'god view' that can be used to show all drivers and users in a city. At an Uber launch party in Chicago, a version of this was used as a party trick, showing the real-time movements of thirty users in New York – without their consent.[14] This highlights the lack of transparency around how data is used by the company – as well as what data it has access to – and reflects some of the claims about a 'toxic' atmosphere within the company.[15]

The geographically tethered model

The platform model has since been adapted to a range of different contexts and types of work. The model for geographically tethered platforms is one that takes existing forms of work that happen in particular places and reorganizes them through a digital platform. There is an ever-growing range of platformized work and services available to us today: from ordering a ride, having food delivered, having your house cleaned, arranging domestic care, getting your clothes washed and ironed, package delivery, to getting your dog walked. Each of these involve recognizable work processes: transportation, takeaways, cleaning, care, laundry and pet sitting existed before digital platforms did.[16] However, the use of smartphone apps to organize both the worker and the customer is a new way to organize work.

Your takeaway cannot make its own way to your door and your dog (probably) cannot take itself for a walk. Geographically tethered work thus tends to require spatial proximities and temporal synchronicities – it needs to happen in a specific place and time. You cannot outsource it to the other side of the planet. What this means is that geographic constraints (i.e. distance, and the local political economy) remain important. In other words, work cannot be completed solely over the internet, free from any geographic constraints (as we will discuss in the next section). Our internet use remains firmly constrained by the internet's physical infrastructure, with fibre optic cables laid across the planet along particular routes – often mirroring earlier communication networks, like shipping and telegraph routes.

The worker may need to be in the right place at the right time to complete a geographically tethered task, but the outsourcing process extends to ensure they are only paid for that productive moment, rather than the waiting time in between demand. Instead of the fleet of delivery drivers paid per hour with expensive equipment provided and maintained by a company, the gig worker is engaged for only the precise slivers of time required to complete a task. This relies upon contractual outsourcing which sidesteps many of the traditional obligations expected of organizations (worker protections and benefits), while still relying – as noted by Scholz (2017a) – on an actual worker.

The development of this model has meant breaking from traditional ways of organizing work. The taxi industry, for example, has many norms and regulations about how a prospective worker becomes a taxi driver. This includes 'the knowledge', the impact of criminal convictions, licensing arrangements, and so on. The geographically tethered model is based on the ability for a pool of potential workers to be called on to meet demand. This has required the development of technology that can do this efficiently, reliably and cost-effectively.

The preconditions that we have argued facilitate the growth of the gig economy can be clearly identified in this model. The changes in political economy have created a deregulated environment in which the platform can position itself as a 'technology company' rather than a cleaning company, taxi company, food delivery company or similar; all while using self-employed independent contractors to do the actual work. Neoliberalism enabled the deregulation of employment to support this model, while also creating an outlet for excess finance capital, allowing it to be poured into these platform companies. The technological factors can also be clearly identified here. In the case of Uber, the platform with its collection of data and automated back-end provides a scalability far beyond existing taxi companies. Building on this, the smartphone app has replaced the physical radio dispatcher as the interface. The use of technology – as well as huge amounts of marketing – provides powerful network effects that draw in both drivers and customers, further spurring this growth. The use of algorithmic management (Lee et al., 2015) keeps the costs low, while providing a new way to effectively manage a geographically dispersed and scalable workforce. Jobs are assigned and evaluated through code and data, without the need for human intervention. There is little chance of feedback, negotiation or the possibility of disputing decisions, resulting in very little transparency for workers. This is a continuation and intensification of the longer processes of outsourcing, minimizing the costs and risks to the platform. At the same time, the social factors that have led many workers to seek more flexible work are pushing many people onto these platforms.

The cloudwork model

Work has always been geographically tethered. As David Harvey (1989: 19) remarked, work is inherently place-based because, in contrast to capital, 'labour-power has to go home every night'. Farmers knew which fields to till, cleaners knew which houses to clean, and factory workers knew which factories to work in. Workers in other words have always had to be physically proximate to the object of their labour. This relationship between workers and place became more complicated once the raw material that workers were creating or transforming was information: something that, with the aid of information and communication technologies can be remotely manipulated.[17]

In other words, the spatial link between workers and the object of their work can be severed. For some types of work, workers need not be physically proximate to the customer, the manager or some of the physical manifestations of the work itself. This means that information-based work can, in theory, be done by anyone, from anywhere, with access to the right technological affordances. When you email customer support or report an image as inappropriate on your favourite social platform, the workers handling those tasks could either be in your city or on the other side of the globe. The untethering of work from place that this has allowed has meant that, for the first time, we potentially have a mass migration of labour without the migration of workers (Standing, 2016).

In order to adequately discuss why our expectations and visions about the relationships between work and economic development may have changed, it is useful to first outline what is and isn't new about digital work. Long, complicated global production networks have always existed. Workers on one side of the planet have laboured to make things for customers on the other without ever coming in contact with them. Two millennia ago, a Chinese silk weaver or Roman farmer might have little idea where the commodities that they made would end up. Today, technology has sped up relationships within global production networks. Workers putting laptops together in factories in Shenzhen could have those machines in shops in Brussels and Berlin by the end of the week. In both examples, it is worth noting that while the site of production can be spread to distant corners of the planet, some service work is necessarily spatially bound to particular places. Silk weavers and laptop assemblers can both perform work thousands of kilometres from European end users. But, until recently at least, shopkeepers are still needed to sell those goods. Some jobs are thus more geographically sticky than others.

Digital platforms have, however, made a lot of work less sticky. As work becomes ever more modularized, commoditized and standardized (Scott, 2001), and as markets for digital work are created, ties between service work and particular places can be severed. While the business process of outsourcing that emerged in the 1990s allowed large companies to take advantage of a 'global reserve army' by moving their call centres to cheap and distant labour markets, cloudwork changes the volume and granularity at which geographically non-proximate work can take place. A small business in New York can hire a freelance transcriber in Nairobi one day and New Delhi the next. No offices or factories need to be built, no local regulations are adhered to, and – in most cases – no local taxes are paid (Graham et al., 2017b; Irani, 2015). The switch in the production network of work happens by simply sending some emails or clicking some buttons on a digital work platform. And, in this way, the employer leaves behind no material traces in the places where it was once an employer. Its effects, however, are far from insignificant. And, as the following chapter will demonstrate, these changing economic geographies of work impact on the livelihoods of workers.

Two of the largest English-language platforms, Upwork and Freelancer, respectively claim to have 12 and 25 million workers signed up on them (Graham and Anwar, 2019). The number of workers signed up on cloudwork platforms is often a multiple of the number who actually find any work. But, if even 7 per cent[18] of those signups ever find jobs, these are staggering numbers on those two platforms alone. Even though certain types of digital work can now – in theory – be commissioned and carried out from anywhere on the planet with an internet connection, it still tends to be characterized by distinct geographies as can be seen in the map in figure 3(a). The map (produced by our colleague Sanna Ojanperä) visualizes a global index of online labour platforms. The index captures the five largest English-language cloud platforms, which represent 70 per cent of the market by traffic.[19] Almost three-quarters of demand for cloudwork on those platforms comes from the US and EU.[20]

We see a very different pattern if we look at the locations of workers (figure 3(b)). According to this data, over two-thirds of the world's crowdworkers live in Asia, and India and Bangladesh alone are home to 41 per cent of the world's population of free-lancers. There is also a significant number of workers from the Global North signed up to cloudwork platforms. The US, for instance, is home to 12 per cent of the world's online freelancers (Ojanperä et al., 2018). Again, the data source is limited in its focus on only English-language platforms. Yet, even with that limitation in mind, it is noteworthy how workers from the Global North and South enter the same planetary market to compete for jobs that largely originate in the Global North (Graham and Anwar, 2019).

It is worth distinguishing between two different types of crowd-work: online freelancing and microwork. Online freelancing, which we have discussed so far, involves the platform as mediator introducing customers and workers often by allowing bidding and negotiation by either party. The work tends to be conducted off-platform, and can involve longer tasks like software development, web design, transcription or translation. The platform profits by taking a cut of the work transaction. Microwork involves the completion of short tasks on a platform interface that tend to be completed quickly, with the worker receiving a piece rate, minus the platform's cut. In a recent ILO study of this kind of work, Berg et al. (2018: xv) found that workers were engaged in a diverse range of tasks, 'including image identification, transcription and annotation; content moderation; data collection and processing; audio and video transcription; and translation.' These tasks were used by clients to 'post bulk tasks', which are split up into small fragments for individual workers to complete.

The Availability of Online Work

Open Vacancies
as a Proportion of the
Global Market from
January to mid-April 2019

- 9.2–39.9%
- 2.1–9.1%
- 0.5–2.0%
- 0.2–0.4%
- 0.02–0.1%
- ≤0.01%
- No Data

Visualisation by Sanna Ojanperä @sanna.ojanpera and Mark Graham @geoplace (geonet.oii.ox.ac.uk).
The visualization uses data from Natural Earth and the Online Labour Index (Kässi, O., & Lehdonvirta, V.
(2018) Online labour index: Measuring the online gig economy for policy and research,
Technological Forecasting and Social Change, 137, pp. 241–248).

Figure 3(a) The availability of cloudwork

Source: https://geonet.oii.ox.ac.uk/blog/mapping-the-availability-of-online-labour-in-2019/

The Availability of Online Workers

Online Workers as a Proportion of the Global Market from January to mid-April 2019

- 6.04–25.5%
- 1.43–6.03%
- 0.34–1.42%
- 0.08–0.33%
- 0.02–0.07%
- ≤0.01%
- No Data

Visualisation by Sanna Ojanperä and Mark Graham @geoplace (geonet.oii.ox.ac.uk).
The visualization uses data from Natural Earth and the Online Labour Index (Kässi, O., & Lehdonvirta, V.
(2018) Online labour index: Measuring the online gig economy for policy and research,
Technological Forecasting and Social Change, 137, pp. 241–248).

Figure 3(b) The location of cloudworkers on the five largest English-language platforms

Source: https://geonet.oii.ox.ac.uk/blog/mapping-the-availability-of-online-labour-in-2019/

Amazon's Mechanical Turk – the world's most well-known microwork platform – refers to these tasks as 'artificial artificial intelligence'. These are tasks that usually rely on a distinctly human ability to interpret things (for instance image recognition or sentiment analysis). These are tasks that might, in theory, be performed by AI, but are cheaper and/or quicker to simply outsource to human workers. For some types of task, it may not be a simple case of humans or artificial intelligence, but rather human microworkers embedded into otherwise automated systems through application programming interfaces (APIs). Here, workers are essentially treated as part of software, algorithms and 'automated' processes. The computer scientist Jaron Lanier (2014: 178) describes this as conjuring up 'a sense of magic, as if you can just pluck results out of the cloud at an incredibly low cost'. Ultimately, this is work that usually requires very little formal training, and – as a result – tends to be poorly paid (Hara et al., 2018). In both cases, what matters to the customer is the final product, not where the actual work was conducted.

Microwork is a clear extension of outsourcing, with roots in crowdsourcing. This term was coined by Howe (2006) to mean 'the act of a company or institution taking a function once performed by employees and outsourcing it to an undefined (and generally large) network of people in the form of an open call'. This provided a way to search for innovation and profitable ideas beyond the boundaries of an organization. However, microwork focuses this into 'a third-generation sourcing ecosystem', that provides a requester with a large pool of accessible workers (Kaganer et al., 2013: 23). The platform provides a way to mediate between customers and workers. This organization of microwork 'relies on dyadic relationships consisting of one buyer, one supplier and a well-defined final deliverable' (Kaganer et al., 2013: 25). This means that the kinds of tasks that are suitable for this platform are short and relatively simple. Larger projects of work can be broken into smaller tasks, but each needs to be completable by an individual working alone. This division of labour allows work to be completed quickly and cheaply. For example, rather than paying a trained expert for transcription, the audio file can be broken down into very small chunks and distributed out across a microwork platform. The quality can be assured by getting each small chunk completed twice and comparing the results. The end result can be achieved much more quickly as each part can be worked on simultaneously. Costs can be kept down by finding workers across the world prepared to work for lowest rates.

If Uber has become the emblematic example of geographically tethered platforms, Amazon Mechanical Turk takes that title for microwork platforms. The name of the platform itself is taken from the Mechanical Turk curiosity. The Mechanical Turk appeared to be a chess-playing automaton; playing against, and beating many prominent figures of the day. However, in its cabinetry, which can be seen in figure 4, was a concealed chess grandmaster who was in fact orchestrating the moves. Rather than being a successful

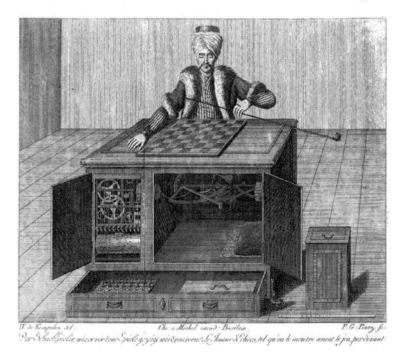

Figure 4 The Mechanical Turk (see https://en.wikipedia.org/wiki/The_Turk)

attempt at artificial intelligence, it was in fact a successful illusion of AI, underpinned by hidden human labour. The platform attempts to do something similar. For the 'requester', a task is put up on the platform and then they pay for and receive the results. The platform mediates between requesters and taskers, ensuring that the two do not have to communicate. Amazon's 'crowd sorcerers work with coolness and the spectacle of innovation to conceal the worker' (Scholz, 2015). In the process, Amazon distributes what it calls HITs (human intelligence tasks) to individual workers. These are separated out from the overall project and workers cannot collaborate on the discrete HITs. Microwork platforms therefore work like a 'black box', a 'system whose workings are mysterious' (Pasquale, 2015: 3). The odd turn of phrase that Amazon uses for tasks – HITs – indicates the connection to artificial intelligence with this kind of work. If Uber's dream is to replace drivers with automated vehicles, the work being conducted on microwork platforms is also key to this process (Gray and Suri, 2019).

It is technically challenging to develop products that are powered by artificial intelligence. The challenge is such that 'some startups have worked out it's cheaper and easier to get humans to behave like robots than it is to get machines to behave like humans' (Solon, 2018). For example, Expensify (an app for business expense management) claimed that its proprietary 'smartscan technology' transcribed receipts. However, scans were being posted as HITs to Amazon Mechanical Turk. As Rochelle LaPlante, a worker on the platform, pointed out: 'I wonder if Expensify SmartScan users know MTurk workers enter their receipts', including 'someone's Uber receipt with their full name, pick-up and drop-off addresses'. Echoing the Mechanical Turk example, Alison Darcy has called this the 'Wizard of Oz design technique', referring to the way the work is hidden behind an interface, like the man hiding behind the projection of the eponymous wizard in the story.[21]

This kind of work is also becoming an increasingly important part of content production on platforms like Facebook and YouTube. While much attention has been paid to the 'produsage' (Bruns, 2008) of users who both use and produce content, often the labour that this relies upon is obscured. A growing number of workers are now engaged in 'commercial content moderation (CCM)' to ensure that users can only upload and view content that is deemed acceptable. As Sarah Roberts (2016), who coined the term, explains, the 'interventions of CCM workers on behalf of the platforms for which they labor directly contradict myths of the Internet as a site for free, unmediated expression'. These workers are engaged in repetitive short tasks which involve viewing 'racist, sexist, homophobic, or sexually or violently graphic content' considered to be too disturbing or unpleasant for users (Roberts, 2016: 150). This work is closer to the often-invisible domestic work being transformed on geographically tethered platforms. In this case, it is the cleaning of content, required for platforms that make money from advertising – after all, advertisers do not want to be associated with the kind of content the CCM workers are deployed to keep off the platform. It is important to note that, in some cases, the tasks done by microworkers are being used to automate machine learning systems: systems that are designed to replace the very workers who train them.

Understanding how platforms work

This chapter began with the example of Uber as the archetypal platform in the gig economy. The Uber model has shown how a digital intermediary can manage the supply and demand of labour, paid for only when utilized by the platform. The existence of a transportation company that owns no vehicles shows how the longer trends of outsourcing have been effectively refigured through the platform to drastically lower the costs of labour. The platform has therefore become a new organizational form, stepping in as an intermediary in increasingly broader kinds of work, collecting both data and a cut of the payments made for services. Uber is an example of this at its most developed – both in terms of scale and use of business practices that seek not only to operate within grey areas of the law, but also to reshape them in the interest of the platform. This is now being replicated in different areas,

Table 1 Governance in the gig economy (inspired by Gereffi et al., 2005)

Buyer	Spatial control	Temporal control	Ability to set rates	Digital legibility	Barriers to entry for workers	Repeat transactions	Degree of explicit coordination
Taxi and delivery work (e.g. Uber)	High	Mixed	High	Mixed	Low	Low	High
Domestic and care work (e.g. SweepSouth)	High	Mixed	High	Low	Low	High	High
Microwork (e.g. Amazon Mechanical Turk)	Low	Low	Low	High	Low	Low	Mixed
Online Freelancing Platform (e.g. Upwork)	Low	Low	Low	Mixed	Mixed	Mixed	Mixed

Note: Because of the huge amount of diversity within the gig economy, this table necessarily over generalizes in almost every category. For instance, there will undoubtedly be cases of geographically-tethered self-employment with high barriers to entry, or online markets with low abilities of workers to set pay rates. However, we would argue that this broad model applies to the majority of work types within each category.

both within geographically tethered work as well as cloudwork. Uber is not the only model in the platform-enabled gig economy. Platforms are entering into increasingly diverse forms of work.

As the geographer Doreen Massey (1984: 8) has argued, organizationally and spatially separating work transformed 'relations between activities in different places, new spatial patterns of social organization, new dimensions of inequality and new relations of domination and dependence'. In order to make sense of this in the gig economy, we have distinguished between the different kinds of platforms and their relative spatial control, temporal control, ability of workers to set pay rates, task discretion, digital legibility, barriers to entry, complexity of labour process, and the degree of explicit coordination and power asymmetry. In table 1, we assess the relationship between these variables. The purpose of this table is not to develop a spectrum of governance types that run from high to low levels of explicit coordination and power asymmetry (as Gereffi et al. (2005) do in their analysis of value chain models). It is rather to illustrate some of the granularity in coordination and power asymmetry within the gig economy, and the diversity of models that can be deployed. There are undoubtedly limits to the spread of platform work, but – as shown in table 1 – there is also a multiplicity of ways of organizing work in the gig economy.

Spatial control

This category refers to the amount of control platforms exert over where workers do their work. Delivery riders and domestic workers have especially low levels of spatial autonomy. Spatial control by the platform is integral to the business model: workers are told which houses to clean, which houses to deliver to, and even which routes to take. Without exerting that control, the platform could not realistically conduct its business.

Cloudwork platforms, in contrast, tend to allow for an extremely high degree of spatial autonomy of their workers. Workers can, in theory, work from anywhere on the planet provided they have a stable internet connection. Cloud platforms also use that spatial freedom as an integral part of their business model. Companies like Upwork or Freelancer are so successful precisely because they bring together a world of workers on a single platform.

Temporal control

On the surface, it might seem as if platforms, by definition, do not exert any temporal control over their workers. Workers are, after all, free to log on and off whenever they choose. However, beyond that, there is a diversity of ways that platforms seek to control when workers work.

Starting from the least amount of control, cloudwork platforms tend not to get involved in when workers log on and off, and instead leave those sorts of negotiations to workers and clients. Workers on geographically tethered platforms likewise are rarely told that they have to work on any given day. In practice, however, platforms have a variety of ways of encouraging workers to be active at particular times. Ride-hailing and delivery platforms use variable rates to increase the available workforce at peak times. Once a worker has accepted a job, platforms then greatly increase the amount of temporal control that they exert. On some platforms, workers are tracked down to the second in order to ensure that work is effectively carried out.

While platforms do not have the ability to use employment contracts to force workers to work at certain times, it is usually a combination of an oversupply of workers and financial incentives to work at certain times that allow platforms to still have some influence on when their workers work. Cleaning, care work and cloudwork also inevitably usually happen on the client's schedule rather than the workers'. By ensuring a greater supply of labour than demand for it, platforms can avoid the messy business of scheduling work. Due to the oversupply of labour on those platforms, cloudworkers often have to complete any jobs that they get on tight schedules. You recall the story of the Ghanaian cloudworker who has to work all night that we mentioned in the introduction, as an example of this. This can mean that, when they find work, it has to be completed very quickly. With geographically tethered workers this often involves a freedom for workers to log on whenever they want, but only certain times of day have enough demand for work. For example, food delivery tends to be clustered around meal times.

Ability to set pay rates

For much geographically tethered work, platforms set rates of pay. Some platforms work on the basis of opaque pricing algorithms that leave workers with no real sense of how that gig would translate into an hourly rate. Others operate complicated bonus and reward schemes that have the same net outcome: workers are unclear about how exactly their time will be compensated.[22] And, in a few cases, there is an ability to accommodate individual workers who seek a higher rate of pay.

Cloudwork platforms tend to operate differently, as workers on those platforms tend to be able to set their own rates as either hourly rates or piece rates. Some platforms do, however, set minimum hourly rates. This act is likely driven less by altruism (or else why still allow some workers in some countries to work for less than their local minimum wage), and more by a desire to increase the commission that they take. Extremely low-wage work is not profitable for the platform for that reason. Even though most cloudwork platforms tend not to set rates, the nature of the marketplace pushes all workers who do not have specialized skills that are in high demand to accepting the going rate for that particular job. As the next chapter will show, going rates can be pushed sharply downwards by the planetary nature of a lot of cloudwork.

Digital legibility

By 'digital legibility', we are referring to the ability of automated processes to read, and ultimately replace key parts of the labour process. The legibility of gig work varies distinctly across the different types of platforms. Tied up in the platform model is the capturing of data from workers and users, and the developing of ways to turn it into a productive resource. For example, with Uber, the actions of workers provide data that is used to further the short-term aims of the platform, while also developing the possibility to replace workers with even cheaper (and more docile) artificial intelligence in the form of self-driving cars. While, in many cases, this level of automation may seem relatively far off, it impacts on the strategy of the platform and also informs the perspective that they take towards workers: why offer a steady and secure employment contract if you would prefer these tasks were automated anyway?

Automation is a concern that is increasingly on the policy agenda throughout the world. For example, in an influential study, Frey and Osborne (2017) analysed the susceptibility of 702 different occupations to computerization. Their key argument is that 47 per cent of employment in the US is at high risk of automation over the next two decades. While this focuses on production, transport and logistics, as well as administrative work, they also point towards the possibilities of automating service work. However, Nedelkoska and Quintini (2018) found that across 32 countries the risk varied significantly, but only 14 per cent of jobs were considered highly automatable. The McKinsey Global Institute (2017) estimates around half of all work could be automated, but again that there would be significant difference by country.

With microwork, many of the tasks may seem ripe for automation, even if at present this is difficult to do. Amazon Mechanical Turk already explicitly frames microwork as 'artificial artificial intelligence'. It is mostly work that could already be automated away (if it were not for an army of cheap labour able to do the same work for less cost than an automated system). Companies are currently experimenting with artificial intelligence solutions to the problems of image recognition, transcription, machine learning, moderation and a range of other needs. Automating those sorts of information-processing tasks, in most cases, entails less risk for the client and end user than, say, automated driving, but there is also less profit to be made by replacing low-wage workers. Domestic and care work, by contrast, is a long way off being automated.

This kind of automation develops at work, emerging out of the economic and power relationships that already exist there

(O'Neil, 2017; Noble, 2018; Eubanks, 2019). Gig work is particularly susceptible to attempts at automation. Transport is an area that is the focus of substantial investment in automation technologies, and many of the sorts of jobs on microwork platforms have already been automated by some companies. With delivery work, some parts of the labour process have already been automated, through the use of GPS-assisted route planning and barcodes or radio-frequency identification (RFID) tagging for inventory management. The second is that in all of these cases, workers are contributing to datasets being used to train artificial replacements. The data generated by drivers contributes to the training sets for self-driving cars, while microwork allows for a much wider range of training data. Often workers will not be aware of the role they are playing, as the tasks are fractured and stripped of their meaning.

Barriers to entry for workers

Many platforms operate with limited barriers to entry for workers, in part because of the relatively low levels of formal training needed for workers to engage in the job. What this means is that platforms can quickly scale up their workforces if needed. Taxi and delivery platforms also have relatively low entry requirements for incoming workers. Workers on many of those platforms need to be able to drive and not have any major criminal convictions, but they do need access to a vehicle. Although cleaning and care work tends to require a high level of ability and skill, its manifestation as platform work is likewise characterized by relatively low barriers to entry.

Online freelancing can incorporate a diverse range of job types: ranging from jobs characterized by relatively low to extremely high complexity. As such, some types of online freelancing can have somewhat higher barriers to entry than other platform jobs. Platform workers rarely have to demonstrate formal qualifications. However, to get jobs in fields such as web development or graphic design, they need to demonstrate both a portfolio of existing work and a high rating on the platform that they work on (which they will only obtain by satisfying their previous clients). Platforms can compensate for relatively higher barriers to entry, and the constraints on the supply of labour that those barriers create, by not constraining the platform to any single local labour market.

Repeat transactions

For many types of platform work, workers tend not to encounter the same clients across gigs. Many microworkers, and some online freelancers, will never actually find out who their clients are. Instead, the client is hidden behind the interface of the platform. Delivery drivers may re-encounter some of the same customers, but those interactions tend to be fleeting. It therefore makes little sense for clients and workers to attempt to disintermediate the platform – repeating their interaction, but without the platform connecting to them. Ride-hail drivers may have long stretches of time with some customers, but – for them too – it makes little sense to attempt to disintermediate the operation of the platform. It is precisely the multi-sided nature of the platform (connecting workers and clients with many potential matches) that is of value to both clients and workers in that case.

With domestic and care work there is an entirely different calculation, however. Here there are both extended interactions between workers and clients and repeated interactions between those same workers and clients: leading to the danger of disintermediation for platforms. For those reasons, platforms such as Homejoy in the US have struggled. Yet some platforms in this line of work still thrive by reducing transaction costs and offering a mechanism for trust to be built between worker and client.

Degree of explicit coordination

We then see that geographically tethered platforms tend to exert a high degree of control over their workforce. Most platforms need to control the locations of workers, manage the time it takes for them to carry out their jobs, set the rates that they receive to do that work. In controlling work in that way, platforms are able to operate with relatively low barriers to entry for their workers. Within these models, however, there are then a range of approaches that grapple with varying degrees of digital legibility and varying levels of repeat interactions between the same workers and clients.

Cloudwork platforms, in contrast, tend to exert less explicit coordination over the labour process. Most platforms do not control the locations of workers, or manage when or how they do their work (even though some offer surveillance tools for clients to monitor their workers). Rate-setting also tends to be left to a negotiation between workers and clients. In most cases, cloudwork platforms attempt to remove barriers to entry for workers. They do this in large part by greatly expanding the geographic scope of where workers can work from and where clients can reach them from, but also by not structuring platform interfaces around formal qualifications or titles. While cloud platforms rarely seek to exert fine-grained control over the labour process, it is rather the contexts and networks that they bring into being that shape much of the nature of work on those platforms.

In sum, there are significant differences in how platforms organize work. However, what is missing so far is the actual experience of workers on these platforms, who – for now at least – do the work that provides the services and creates value for the platforms. It is to their experiences and the ways that they interact with these different forms of governance that we now turn.

3

What is it like to work in the gig economy?

In this chapter we turn to focus on the experience of workers in the gig economy. The preceding chapters have examined where the gig economy came from, discussed the debates that surround it and outlined the business models and operations that drive platforms. However, we cannot hope to fully understand the gig economy without also considering the experiences of the workers who support it. Trying to make sense of it without focusing on workers is like studying astronomy without ever looking up at the stars. And of course, the deep and ingrained knowledge of what it is like to work in the gig economy is already out there, held in the lived experience of workers across the world on many different platforms.

Drawing on extensive interview and ethnographic data, we turn to the voices of workers who do this work every day, and with whom we interact in both visible and invisible ways. We cannot claim to represent the voices of all gig workers in this chapter – it is far too short for that. The experience of working in the gig economy necessarily varies by place, by platform and by the myriad positionalities that each worker brings to the job. There are, as Alexandrea Ravenelle (2019: 1) has argued, 'strugglers', 'survivors' and 'success stories' in the gig economy. But by highlighting a range of case studies and examples that reoccur in the gig economy, we can begin to sketch out the good and bad of the gig economy.

Delivery work

Geographically tethered forms of gig work are often the most visible in major cities, as workers need to be in particular places to complete the work. The rapid growth of food delivery platforms has meant that large numbers of workers have been drawn into working as riders on bicycles, motorbikes and mopeds via platforms like Deliveroo. For many workers, the process of making money on a platform like Deliveroo is straightforward and it offers a particular kind of flexibility.

The desire for flexibility is something expressed by many of the workers we have interviewed, as well as one of the preconditions we have identified for the gig economy in chapter 1. For example, Mumit,[1] who drives a motorbike in London for Deliveroo, explained his choice to work on the platform: 'When I got insured on my bike I was like what do I do? I need to find myself a gig, I don't know what I'm doing now, you know, so then I thought ok, bikes [are] my passion, I wanted to make money riding my bike, so I found like a delivery job.' The flexibility of the job was a draw; however, it resulted in Mumit driving for 'six days a week. On a Sunday, my longest day, I do about from ten o'clock to half-eleven in the evening, so thirteen and a half hours. Mondays I do quarter to twelve to half-eleven. The rest of the week I do from five to half-eleven and Saturday is my day off!' This kind of schedule is common for a motorbike/moped driver, in which they need to work a large percentage of peak hours – over Friday, Saturday and Sunday evenings – in order to get access to priority shift booking. The fewer peak hours a driver works, the less access they have for shift booking, meaning they then have less flexibility in choosing when to work. The 'flexibility' of the work then becomes more nuanced – and often dependent on working large numbers of hours per week.

The platform's use of self-employed or 'independent contractor' status means that Mumit, like tens of thousands of drivers across the UK, does not have an employment contract with Deliveroo. The result is that while workers can choose when to work, they need to work the peak meal times of lunch and dinner to make enough money – as well as the majority of Friday, Saturday and Sunday evenings. This echoes Karl Marx's (1976: 272) observation that we discussed earlier about workers being doubly free. This 'freedom' and 'flexibility' is not sufficient for the workers themselves. For example, Alejandro explained that he used to be a chef before working for Deliveroo. In that job, he:

> had a contract, holiday pay sick pay ... with Deliveroo there isn't anything, it's a problem. If I have an accident it's my problem, the company only care about if you deliver the order and that's it. I feel less secure absolutely. I feel alone with the company, you feel like you are a self-employed because you don't have bosses but at the same time Deliveroo is your boss, you can't see anybody but you work for a company.

Alejandro's self-employed status means that the usual benefits and social security are not available to him, with only the wage being paid to the worker. This is far from the promise presented by Deliveroo in their advertising to new riders. Mumit, who at the time of interview had already had bikes stolen, written off in accidents, and had broken bones while working, explained that when things go wrong:

> Deliveroo don't care, it's got nothing to do with them, because you're an independent contractor so you have to deal with your own things. They don't care, they'll sign you off for the shift until you can get back, they'll say get back in touch with us and that's all through the call centre as well, not through a person who's ... even pretending to give a fuck [laughter].

For Alejandro, the result of working under these conditions was that:

we feel scared sometimes. I am young, I don't have any family to care for, it's not all that bad for me short term. But long term you're scared, you're scared. If I want to go holidays I need to keep money; if I crash or broke my leg so I can't work. If I can't work I can't pay the rent, I can't go holidays, so it's a process that's quite hard.

Alejandro – like many of the Deliveroo drivers we have spoken to – complained that 'we are not really self-employed'. At the time of writing in 2019, the Independent Workers union of Great Britain (IWGB) had brought a case to the CAC (Central Arbitration Committee), in which Deliveroo intervened and successfully argued that the drivers should not have worker status. This means that the platform has, so far, successfully freed itself from the responsibility to cover workers in the event of something going wrong. This is particularly important in driving work, given a recent survey of gig economy drivers, riders and their managers finding that '42% said they had been involved in a collision where their vehicle had been damaged and 10% of the total sample said that someone had been injured as a result and this was usually themselves' (Christie and Ward, 2018: 4–5). Furthermore, 'Three quarters of respondents (75%) said that there had been occasions while working when they have had to take action to avoid a crash.' The piece-rate arrangement also means drivers are 'chasing jobs', taking risks in order to get more work, which 'increases the exposure to risk'. Christie and Ward's (2018: 5) conclusion is that 'these faceless digital brokers take no responsibility for the health and safety of the people who accrue income for them.' This had fatal consequences for Pablo Avendano, working for Caviar (a food delivery platform) in the US. He was killed after being hit by another vehicle while working in heavy rain in Philadelphia. The callous non-response of the platform in response to Pablo's death was summed up by one of his friends: 'like risk and liability, Caviar seems to want to outsource even the emotional labor of mourning to its independent contractors and society as whole.'[2]

Despite this clear tragedy, it is important to stress that worker experiences of delivery platforms are not all negative. As Mumit explained, at Deliveroo: 'the work itself is really good, because it is the algorithm that's the boss, you do get that kind of a sense of freedom, even though it's not really [freedom].' He goes on to explain that because there is 'no interaction with Deliveroo' other than through the app and emails, this means no supervisor standing over your shoulder telling you what to do, or the experience of being 'bossed around' by a manager. Similarly, Fred, a Deliveroo rider in London argued that it is 'actually like a reasonable shit job because that illusion of freedom is really strong like you do kind of feel like your own boss because we can all stand around and talk shit about Deliveroo as much as we like'. Unlike other forms of low-paid service work, 'there's no reason to be extra nice to people like you're not selling anything, you're not selling yourself so there's no emotional labour in it.' On these platforms, the tip is mainly paid in the app before the delivery is actually made. While there are sometimes cash tips, these are rare. Compared to work in call centres, hospitality, and so on, this means not having to bring emotions to work and manage them throughout the shift, with all the stress that entails (Woodcock, 2017).

There is still the experience of surveillance for drivers, whether through the location-tracking on the app, or the visibility on the roads. For example, in December 2018 in India, a driver for Zomato (a food delivery platform) was spotted eating some of a customer's takeaway before delivering it. The video was widely shared on social media, leading to the driver being deactivated. As one commentator, Dushyant Shekhawat, noted: 'what made the man take a bite was, quite possibly, a horribly unfair system that had him working ungodly hours, to deliver food he could never afford for himself, to people who likely never tip.'[3] In our fieldwork in India we have found that many drivers work twelve hours a day, seven days a week, often in dangerous traffic conditions – something also echoed in our interviews in South Africa. In one group interview in Bangalore, drivers recounted how they had started receiving 60 rupees per delivery, which had then fallen to 40 rupees, and most recently down to 30 rupees.[4] At no point had the platform negotiated these changes – instead, they were announced to the drivers. At the end of the interview, we asked drivers what one thing they would like to be improved on the platform. They all replied 'more money', and when we asked if there was anything else, they shook their heads and pointed their fingers upward: 'more money'.

Taxi work

One of the key differences with delivering passengers rather than packages or takeaways is that there is a more direct interaction with customers. With delivery work, the customer can choose to tip the delivery rider through the app at the point of sale, meaning the interaction at the doorstep happens after the decision to tip, taking away the pressure of a positive service interaction. However, with platforms like Uber, the decision to tip happens at the end of the journey after the customer decides on the quality of the experience. This is accompanied with the use of a star rating system, which can determine whether or not a driver can continue to work on the platform. The rating system does not allow for much of a choice, given it has become customary for both drivers and customers to give five stars. This means dropping below that rating can put the driver at risk. On Uber, going below 4.7 in many cities can risk 'deactivation' of the driver – that is, being fired. This makes drivers vulnerable to demanding riders, as 'only a small number of complaints can lead to the driver losing their livelihood' (Slee, 2015: 73).

James Farrar – a co-founder of UPHD (United Private Hire Drivers), the Uber driver branch of IWGB – has explained what this process looks like in practice in an interview with James Temperton for Wired.[5] One Friday night Farrar picked up three passengers in London. As they had been drinking, they were demanding and difficult passengers, an experience for the driver just 'like any other Friday night as an Uber driver'. One passenger opened a door at a junction so she could vomit onto the road. Farrar stopped the journey, attempted to file a report to Uber, and would not set off again straight away. The group called another Uber which arrived. Following from his recent experience, James decided to warn the new Uber driver – something which his now ex-passengers opposed. One of them attacked Farrar, pushing and shouting anti-Irish abuse at him, and damaging his car. Due to his concerns about Uber taking the passenger's side – something reported by many drivers – he called the police to report what had happened, attempting to protect himself against a complaint from the passengers. As they had booked through Uber, he could only say it was 'my customer, but I don't know the name, or the address, but I'll ask Uber for it'. Uber refused to provide details for reasons relating to data privacy. Uber then refused to release the information without a court order.

What this event highlights is that despite their classification as self-employed, an Uber driver has little control over situations where something goes wrong. In response, Farrar contacted a law firm and began the process of challenging Uber on the basis of being misclassified, a process that at the time of writing in 2019 has already taken in excess of three years.[6] Farrar is not the only person to complain about the power passengers hold over Uber drivers. As Yaseen Aslam – another co-founder of UPHD – has explained, he had to 'keep my rating high to keep my job'. The result was 'always' being 'nervous of getting very low ratings from customers as it wouldn't take that many one-star ratings to put me at risk of deactivation. I felt that this system was inhumane.'[7]

These kinds of concerns are not only about the stress of deactivation, but can also have serious ramifications for the safety of drivers on the road, as already noted for delivery work. For example, in South Africa, Uber has faced serious – and sometimes violent – opposition from traditional metered taxi drivers. This risk of violence only increased as Uber began allowing cash payments to encourage users who did not have access to credit cards. While this grew the user base, it also exposed drivers to increased risks as they were now expected to carry cash. Whilst a limited number of taxis had existed beforehand, in cities like Johannesburg this meant there were now many potential robbery targets driving the streets, which could be ordered into dangerous situations via the app.[8] What followed was a spate of robberies and hijackings. Some of those attacks led to the murder of drivers.[9] A demand of almost all

Uber drivers that we spoke to in South Africa was for the platform to introduce positive identification for customers – something it already requires of drivers, whose photographs are shown to customers when they order a ride. Bolt, the rival platform in South Africa, allows cash journeys and even less identification from passengers – just a mobile phone number that can be obtained from a throwaway sim card. Many of the drivers we spoke to discussed how they could earn more with Bolt as the platform takes a smaller percentage fee, but the issues with safety made working for that platform much more of a risk, particularly at night.

The lack of any collective voice – or even individual channels – has meant that platforms like Uber and Bolt experience little, if any, pressure to implement changes. Even without the risk of robberies, many Uber drivers in South Africa have had their earnings significantly eroded due to rising petrol prices in the country. Uber and Bolt workers cannot change their rates to cover the additional costs, left only with the algorithmically determined price. Moreover, in South Africa many of the trips are short, reflecting users' fears of public safety. Drivers do not know how far a customer wants to travel until they have picked them up, as the destination is only revealed after this point. Drivers therefore complain that waiting for, travelling to, and carry out short trips can often cost as much – or in some cases more – than the fee the driver will receive. In both of these cases, self-employed drivers should have much more control over their work than they currently experience. This has led to protests and wildcat strikes in response to fuel price rises. As one striking worker explained to Times Live (a South African newspaper): 'at this time last year, after a hard day's work and after all expenses such as fuel had been paid, I could earn R3,500 weekly ... now, some weeks, drivers are barely getting R500 a week' (approximately £28 a week).[10]

Despite the wild claim that Uber drivers in New York earn $90,000 per year,[11] the reality across the world is that the platform is putting immense pressure on drivers' incomes, both on and off the platform. As James Farrar testified in the Central London Employment Tribunal in 2016 'in some months he earned as little as £5 per hour, well below the current national minimum wage for over-25s of £7.20' – the minimum wage at the time.[12] The latest case concerns claims that the '40,000 drivers are allowed almost £11,000 in wages and more than £8,000 in holiday pay', as Uber 'refuses to recognize a two-year-old ruling entitling them to holiday pay, a minimum wage and rest breaks'.[13]

In our discussions with Uber drivers across London, as well as in other parts of the world, they have confirmed that earnings are low. However, despite the evidence that making a living as an Uber driver is difficult, large numbers of workers are still choosing to sign up to the platform, something noted by author Tom Slee (2015: 67), who asks 'if the pay is really so poor, why do so many people drive for Uber?' The answer, he says, is that:

> For those who have a car, driving for Uber is a way of converting that capital into cash; some underestimate the costs involved with full-time driving; for some the flexibility is a boon; for many, driving for Uber offers what taxi driving has offered for years – a job that requires little skill and has a low cost of entry is better than nothing. And as Uber has cut into the demand for taxis in many cities, individual taxi driver income has fallen, leaving Uber as the best alternative.

In this way, Uber has become the quintessential example of gig work – that is, the idea of driving people around in between other jobs, adding another 'gig' to the worker's repertoire, while putting the asset of the car to profitable use. As Slee notes, it can indeed be difficult for workers to estimate the costs involved with full-time driving, particularly with fuel prices, but also the prevalence of what is effectively sub-prime car financing, along with complex estimations of car value depreciation. For a sense of the kind of calculations that drivers are faced with to make it in the gig economy, The Uber Game, published in *The Financial Times*, provides players with some interactive insights about how difficult it is to make money as an Uber driver,[14] particularly drawing attention to the hidden costs.

The point about cutting into the demand for taxis in many cities has also meant that Uber has changed the experience of work for taxi drivers who have never signed up to their app. In New York, which has operated a medallion system for limiting the number of taxis, Uber is having a deeply disruptive effect. At the start of 2018, Doug Schifter, a taxi driver in New York, shot himself in front of the City Hall in Manhattan. In a Facebook post he explained how he was having to work for over 100 hours a week to survive, while in the 1980s he had worked forty hours per week. The value of taxi medallions in New York had a peak of US$1 million before Uber, which is now down to US$500,000 and is continuing to fall. This means that some drivers have taken on debt at the peak value for something now worth half that, without the same availability of work to repay that debt. Schifter had lost his health insurance and run up debt, and declared he would no longer work for 'chump change'.[15] Similarly, Bhairavi Desai, the founder of the New York Taxi Workers Alliance, reports having received calls in 2017 from a community of Dominican taxi drivers, explaining how dire the situation had become, with two drivers also having killed themselves.

Domestic and care work

Domestic and care work platforms follow the model of acting as an intermediary between workers and customers, taking a cut from the worker's payment, while also sometimes charging additional fees on top. In this case, they can involve workers cleaning houses or providing care on demand, for example. There is a longer tradition of this in some parts of the world, whereas elsewhere new demand is being created. However, the high-profile nature of transport and delivery platforms, particularly Uber and Deliveroo, means that they often dominate discussions around the gig economy. The 'Uber for X' shorthand gives a good sense of how that model has come to dominate this kind of work. However, despite Uber (and Deliveroo) becoming the go-to examples, this can lead to us forgetting the other kinds of location-specific work. Ticona and Mateescu (2018) have argued that the narrative of 'Uberization' fails to capture how domestic work platforms operate. Domestic work is often described as 'invisible'; excluded from many employment protections, often carried out by migrant women workers, and lacking collective bargaining (Pollert and Charlwood, 2009). This lack of focus also points towards a gendered bias in the literature that focuses on forms of work that men are most likely to be involved in (Ticona and Mateescu, 2018). While the bulk of the research on digital labour has ignored domestic and care work platforms, the voices of workers across the gig economy are mostly absent too. Our research has so far focused on transportation and delivery, as well as microwork and online freelancing, but we have been conducting fieldwork with a range of platforms in India and South Africa since the start of 2018, including both domestic and care work platforms.

Anderson (2000: 1–2) argues that there are two factors that determine the living and working conditions of domestic workers. First, their relationship to the state, with regard to their immigration status. Second, their relationship to the employer, and whether they 'live in' or not. With work platforms, the former can become problematic when workers become more visible to the state through the need to present documents to register, while in the latter case they only visit the employer's home for a short period of time so the relationship to the employer is much shorter. However, unlike the clear labour (or task) objectives involved in driving or delivering food, domestic work can be far more complex. It often lacks specific job descriptions or definitions, as Anderson (2000: 15) found when interviewing domestic workers, who, when asked what they did, would frequently say 'everything'.

There are approximately 67 million domestic workers across the world, with women making up 80 per cent of the workforce (Hunt and Machingura, 2016: 5). In many countries this kind of work is being transformed by platforms like Care.com, Handy and SweepSouth. As Ticona and Mateescu (2018) explain, these platforms 'formalize employment relationships through technologies that increase visibility'. Workers create profiles and receive feedback and ratings, using this as the basis for repeat work. Care. com operates in twenty countries, with 12.7 million 'caregivers'

(Care.com, 2018). This is a significantly larger number of workers than the 3.9 million claimed by Uber.

The risk of complete automation is not so obvious with this kind of work. As Dalla Costa and James (1971: 11) have noted, 'a high mechanization of domestic chores doesn't free any time for the woman. She is always on duty, for the machine doesn't exist that makes and minds children.' Ticona and Mateescu (2018) point out that domestic work is both 'among the fastest growing and perhaps the most resistant to automation'. Large numbers of workers are being drawn in – still doing the same kind of domestic work, but now mediated via a platform rather than employment agency. Initial research on these kinds of platforms has found that there can be some positive outcomes for domestic workers, including 'choice over working times, tracking of hours worked and wages earnt, and potentially better remuneration compared with other forms of domestic work', while also identifying 'low and insecure incomes, discrimination, further entrenchment of unequal power relations within the traditional domestic work sector, and the erosion of established labour and social protections as key challenges' (Hunt and Machingura, 2016: 5). The increased visibility of domestic workers on platforms can facilitate both the positives and the negatives.

What few findings there are, however, are beginning to draw attention to the experiences of this kind of work, giving voice to workers who have been marginalized both historically and structurally. In Hunt and Machingura's (2016) important research on domestic work platforms, they interviewed workers in South Africa. One worker they spoke to, Busi, explained that SweepSouth (a major domestic work platform):

> takes R13 [\$0.90] for every R38 [\$2.63] ... per hour. So, for example, if I work for three hours, instead of getting R120 [\$8.29], all I get is R75 [\$5.18]. On that R75, I have to cater for my own transport no matter how far the place I go and work is. Usually, that only leaves me with R20 [\$1.38] [for the whole job].

The experience of working piecemeal by the hour meant that Busi had to travel to different neighbourhoods, often those she was not familiar with. Given the limited public transport in South African cities like Johannesburg, this meant she would often have to walk and could arrive too late to make the appointment. At the time of the study, the minimum wage for domestic workers was R13.39 per hour (in metro areas, working less than 27 hours per week), which is less than the minimum wage for all other workers (Hunt and Machingura, 2016). While SweepSouth paid above the minimum wage, the worker still needs to take into account costs involved in the work. For example, Busi explained:

> this is really sad for me because I have a family to look after, I am a single parent. At the end of the week when I look at how much I have worked for, I ask myself why I am killing myself like this. (Quoted in Hunt and Machingura, 2016: 23)

This experience is also detailed by another worker, Susan, who was also interviewed by Hunt and Machingura (2016: 24):

> I came from Zimbabwe straight into someone's home as a domestic worker. I worked as a full-time house maid ... When I realized that the money was too little ... I moved over to the next person ... until I realized that stay-in jobs are not well-paying. I started doing part-time jobs [through the platform] and that really paid me well because I would get R200–R250 [$14–$18] per day. So I brought my children from Zimbabwe because I could now afford to take care of them and send them to school here. I could also even afford the day care course I was talking about. But honestly, it's very hard because all the [extra] money goes back to transport, airtime, bundles and some [clients] are rude and delay payment, or lie that you have stolen something, among other things.

This kind of work is clearly 'very hard' and low paid, and workers also lack formal channels to improve their situation. To focus on South Africa again, while there are relevant unions like the South African Domestic Services and Allied Workers Union (SADSAWU), they are yet to make any major inroad into organizing these platform workers. SweepSouth employs, or rather contracts, a workforce that is overwhelmingly black African and female. They have an estimated 8,500 registered workers in South Africa. A recent survey by SweepSouth indicates some of the structural barriers these workers face (SweepSouth, 2018). For example, in their survey of 500 domestic workers, they reported that 84 per cent were the sole breadwinners in their family, and on average supported three dependents. Thirteen per cent reported that they 'suffered physical or verbal abuse from someone they worked for'. There is also a separate lower minimum wage for domestic workers, which means that these workers are only entitled to a minimum of R2,625 (£145) per month, rather than the R3,500 minimum that other workers are entitled to. However, the surveyed workers spent on average R900 on food, R400 on electricity, R500 on school fees, R1,000 on rent, and R100 on airtime for a total of R2,900 per month (SweepSouth, 2018). However, this does not include the substantial transportation costs that these workers need to travel to appointments, which according to the research company Numbeo, could be as much as R500 per month (quoted in SweepSouth, 2018). Aisha Pandor (the founder and CEO of SweepSouth) has argued that 'it's easy to say let's increase salaries across the board but the reality is that we face high levels of unemployment in the country.'[16] With the example of domestic work, low wages also combine with the historical undervaluing of this kind of activity, resulting in damaging outcomes for workers – now mediated via an app.

Microwork

In a different vein to either taxi, delivery or domestic and care work, many people are now finding and completing work through the internet, without the need to be in any particular place. In the US, up to 5 per cent of the population have made money from a work platform by completing digital tasks. This figure rises for workers under 30, and is higher than the equivalent figures for taxi driving (2 per cent) or delivery and cleaning (1 per cent) (Smith, 2016).

In most other places, it is difficult to get hard statistics on the number of people engaged in microwork. Microwork is usually carried out behind closed doors in the home. As such, it is typically hidden from the end user, making it difficult to get a sense of what its value chains look like and how the job of microwork is structured and organized. Whenever we use a digital service, product or even an algorithm that was trained using digital labour, there is almost no way to know whether an exhausted worker is behind it; whether they get laid off if they become sick or get pregnant; whether they are spending twenty hours a week just searching for work; how precarious their source of income is; or whether they are being paid an unfairly low wage.

In the Global North, this kind of work is growing within a context of deindustrialization, becoming an option for people who may have seen alternative kinds of jobs disappearing. As Alana Semuels (2018) has uncovered in interviews with microworkers in the US, this kind of work is increasing. One of her interviewees, Erica, explained that she started working for Amazon Mechanical Turk after struggling to find work in her 'economically struggling town'. She noted that 'here, it's kind of a dead zone. There's not much work.' In the county where she lives, only half of people over the age of 16 have a job, and a quarter are below the poverty line. Erica spends around thirty hours a week completing simple tasks, surveys and questionnaires, earning around US$4–5 per hour, but often much less. Much of the working time can be unpaid. For example, Erica recounts examples of tasks that requesters claim will take twenty minutes, but that actually take an hour. Often this can only be discovered after putting in enough time that it is worth completing anyway. Erica explains, 'I've felt so ripped off that I've walked away and cried.' A significant amount of unpaid time can also be spent by workers simply searching for and applying for jobs.[17] Another interviewee, Valerie, explains that she started working for Mechanical Turk after her car battery died, forcing her to work from home to try to make the money for repairs.[18]

A question that might come to mind with these stories is how workers can be paid so little to do these tasks? As with geographically tethered work, microworkers are organized as independent contractors, rather than workers or employees. So, when Erica receives US$4 an hour, which is US$3.25 below the federal minimum wage of US$7.25, Amazon is not breaching any local laws (Semuels, 2018). Emerging evidence shows that the stories of Erica and Valerie are not outliers, but rather representative of the trend for earnings on Mechanical Turk. In a recent study, it was demonstrated that workers earned a median hourly wage of only around US$2 per hour. At the upper end, only 4 per cent of workers earned more than the US$7.25 per hour federal minimum wage in the US. As the average requester paid over $11 per hour (indicating that requesters who pay much less also offer far more work), this demonstrates how the actual hourly wage is lower, taking into account the amount of unpaid work needed to find and complete the job (Hara et al., 2018).

On platforms like this, it is not possible to be productive (in the sense of doing paid work) for 100 per cent of a worker's available time. Significant time is spent searching for tasks, or working on tasks that do not convert into pay. The ability of requesters to 'reject work that does not meet their needs' is built into the Amazon platform, and 'enables wage theft' (Irani and Silberman, 2013). As another study has found, workers who used the online rating website Turkopticon to evaluate requesters on Amazon Turk, could avoid wage theft, given requesters who were badly rated committed wage theft about five times more than highly rated employers. For workers, choosing to only work for those higher rated requesters would mean making 40 per cent more (Benson et al., 2015). This highlights how wage theft is, as Irani and Silberman (2013) have argued, a key part of these platforms.

For those of us who have never worked for a microwork platform, it can be hard to imagine what the day-to-day work is like. Eric Limer, a reporter who decided to try Amazon Mechanical Turk for a story assignment, described how the experience is one of fractured and hard-to-understand tasks. In his first task – an experience he says stayed with him long afterwards – he was asked to track people on social media, trying to link user accounts across different platforms. In another odd task, he was requested to perform expressions in front of a webcam to help 'teach ...

computers how to detect these kind of expressions'.[19] Across a range of these experiences, Limer explains that

> If I've made Mechanical Turk sound like a disturbing hole that sucks up countless dazed hours clicking away pondering the world as a strange unimaginable shape, that's because it is. Or, it's a relatively fun way to make a couple bucks playing around on the internet ... I did this shit for hours. It's addictive! Mechanical Turk is like gambling's alternate universe cousin. It's a bizarre cephalopodan slot machine, a thousand-armed bandit that pays you for the trouble of pulling one of its many strange levers. I found it alarmingly easy to slip into a Turking daze. Each strange task leaves you with a brief glimpse of some larger whole, and it's easy to find yourself looking for just one more.

It leverages the 'gamification' that is a feature of many forms of work today (Woodcock and Johnson, 2018) in order to encourage people to work for an amount that may not hit minimum wage.

In the process, it unveils parts of modern society that are often hidden: the work that goes on behind the scenes to develop AI and run services that many of us rely on. In some cases, the work that is being requested can be much more sinister than the tasks that Limer describes. For example, in his ongoing PhD research, Adam Badger (2018) has traced where some of his writing tasks have ended up. For one, he was asked to rewrite an article for Russia Today on Russia stockpiling gold, with the task setter noting that 'our readers are into conspiracy theories'. The payment for this was US$3, with an additional US$1 for an image to go with it, plus a bonus of US$1 for 'exceptional work'. As Badger explained, as 'a writer, lefty, and general critic of the role of the internet and the press on our contemporary psyche, the job made me deeply uncomfortable'. Ethics is not something that most microworkers get much of an opportunity to reflect upon when selecting work, particularly as 'once the tasks are done, they also often shoot-off into the ether with no follow-up apart from the payment (if you're lucky).' However, in this case, Adam was able to track down the article afterwards as he could search for parts of the text via Google. The result was finding the article published under someone else's name, and Adam explained, 'if that wasn't creepy enough, there was a video made for the "Alternative News Network" (ew...) which is just a narrated version of my article as read by a robot from the dystopian future' (Badger, 2018).

Another glimpse into the experiences of microworkers can be found with the 'Dear Mr. Bezos' letters organized by Mechanical Turk workers to the founder and CEO of Amazon. This followed an article in *Business Insider*, which noted that 'Jeff Bezos may run Amazon and he may be a billionaire, but he is very accessible to his customers with an easy-to-find email address, jeff@amazon.com.'[20] Through Dynamo,[21] a workers campaign was organized to send emails to Bezos with three aims: first, to point out that 'Turkers [workers on Mechanical Turk] are human beings, not algorithms, and should be marketed accordingly'; second, that 'Turkers should not be sold as cheap labour, but instead skilled, flexible labour which needs to be respected'; and third, that 'Turkers need to have a method of representing themselves to Requesters and the world via Amazon'. In each of these emails, which can still be found on the internet,[22] the experiences and concerns of these workers are made clear, all starting with 'Dear Mr. Bezos' – or close to it. For example:

Dear Mr. Bezos
I am a Turker: middle age, entrepreneur, university student, mom, wife, reliant on my mTurk income to keep my family safe from foreclosure. I don't Turk for $1.45 per hour nor do I live in a developing country, I am a skilled and intelligent worker, and I Turk as my main source of income and it is currently my chosen career. I am a human being, not an algorithm, and yet Requesters seem to think I am there just to serve their bidding. They do not respect myself and my fellow Turkers with a fair wage, and in fact say that we should be thankful we get anything near to minimum wage for the 'easy' work we do. Searching for work all day isn't easy. Having to find and install scripts to become more efficient isn't easy. Dealing with unfair rejections isn't easy. Being a Turker isn't easy.
Kristy Milland (Turkernation Forum)
...

Hi Jeff,

I am from India, I am so grateful that you build such great platform for online jobs, it makes my life little more easier than others.

I am not just writing for me or Indians, but every single turker who are so much depended on income from AMT. It is time to upgrade your system, countries other than India and USA, only have payment as gift vouchers, which is not enough, please try to introduce new ways to get paid or improve Amazon Payments. If you can introduce Direct Deposit methods for us, it will be great.

Create a better platform for the workers, AMT need both Requesters and Workers, so make it equal. Try an inbuilt review system for every Requester, so that we can avoid cheaters.

And lastly, introduce a minimum wage system, all of the workers in AMT are well educated and experienced people, we deserve the right pay for quality work we provide.

That's all from me, once again thanks for everything you have done for us.

Bayon

In sum, microwork can often feel like the ultimate in alienated labour. Workers are rarely told why they are asked to do what they do. Work and workers are treated as entirely interchangeable, and disembedded from local laws and norms. As a result, platform-based microwork tends to be traded in small chunks, with workers given a take-it-or-leave-it offer on whether or not to accept any given job. Microwork platforms offer the promise of maximum productivity for clients who can pay workers only for the minutes (or even seconds) that they spend on the job. For workers, despite the fact that many workers rely on microwork as their primary source of income, there is no illusion that microwork offers a sustainable career path.

Microwork, at its essence, harnesses many of the computational and sensory skills innate to the human brain. Many workers are hired not because they have a deep domain knowledge, a long career, or formal qualifications in a particular domain of work or knowledge. They are, rather, hired because they are a human being willing to perform a relatively interchangeable task for a certain amount of money. And yet, despite its reliance on its workers' core human-ness, it remains the fact that microwork is severely lacking in humanity and attention to human dignity. Microwork, in its present state, offers a bleak look into a world of commodified jobs that are sliced up, and shipped off to a microwork platform, with little attention or care to the individuals carrying them out.

Online freelancing

The rise of online freelancing offers a case that is unprecedented in human history. While the practice is a clear extension of offshoring and outsourcing for service jobs, we now see global labour arbitrage happening at a scale that was never before possible. At the time of writing, the world's largest freelancing platform, Freelancer. com[23] claims to have connected 'over 30,325,814 employers and freelancers globally from over 247 countries, regions, and territories', and their Twitter account lists their location as 'everywhere'. Upwork.com, which hosts 12 million registered workers, likewise talks about their worker pool as being global in scope: 'online work can happen wherever there's a reliable Internet connection – an office, home, café, or rooftop. This also means you can choose who you work with, among a larger pool of people from around the globe.' Online freelancing is a broad term that can encapsulate all manner of jobs. Workers writing essays, doing 'lead generation', designing presentations, building websites, working as personal assistants, and carrying out all manner of other jobs all get their work through online freelancing platforms that allow workers and clients to connect in a planetary labour market (Graham and Anwar, 2019).

For many workers, the planetary scale of the market affords workers a significant amount of freedom in choosing where to work from, and in many cases allows them to escape from relatively constrained local labour markets. There are workers in places like Manila in the Philippines or Lagos in Nigeria who simply want an escape from the horrendous local traffic conditions (it is not uncommon to hear stories of three-hour commutes to work in both places). Working as online freelancers allows those workers to work from home or nearby cafes or Wi-Fi hotspots.

Other workers sign up because there are simply not enough good jobs close to home. Examples include young Kenyans who struggle to find any work because of the extremely high youth unemployment rates in the country; Palestinians with few options because of the economic entanglement of their economy;[24] and migrants around the world who lack the requisite work permits to find jobs locally. For all of those groups, online freelancing opens up opportunities that would not otherwise be there for them. Online freelancing allows workers to escape some of the fundamental constraints of the local labour market, and access jobs that would likely otherwise not be available to them.

Especially important to many workers is that salaries for online freelancing jobs can often be higher than wages they would receive in the local labour market. Angel, a transcriber in Manila, left a job in nursing in order to work for American and European clients that could be found on a large freelancing website. The pay that Angel received transcribing text was significantly higher than wages for local nurses. So, despite having spent years training to be a nurse, Angel moved to solely focus her working hours on transcription. Similar stories exist in low- and middle-income countries around the world, and the ability to earn wages that are significantly higher than those that can be obtained locally is an alluring draw for many people and leads people to forge entirely new career paths.

The freedom to work from wherever you want is especially appealing to young women across the Global South because of the ability to work from home, combining childcare duties with work. This seemed especially productive when other family members (parents, siblings and occasionally spouses) could look after children during work hours. While such arrangements are undoubtedly empowering for many, it is worth paying attention to the ways in which crowdwork is essentially subsidized by the reproductive labour of the rest of the household. Many other workers choose to freelance from public spaces in order to take advantage of free Wi-Fi (in most low- and middle-income countries, few people have unmetered internet connections at home). Yet others work from schools, universities and physical offices in order to take advantage of the computers and fixed infrastructures in those places. In all these cases, the infrastructure, connectivity, childcare and other domestic work that are carried out in the household are not treated as business expenses, and yet all serve to facilitate the freelancing that is carried out.

For every worker who realizes significant opportunities in online freelancing, there are many more whose goals go unrealized. A study of Upwork.com shows that globally, less than 7 per cent of people who register for jobs are ever able to secure one (Graham and Anwar, 2019). This oversupply of labour power is fiercely experienced by workers.

It is a rare online freelancer who feels that they have significant bargaining power in relation to the clients who source their work (Wood et al., 2018). Workers are well aware of the fact that if they try to raise their rates, there are thousands of people from around the world who are willing to do the same job, sometimes for a fraction of their own wage (Wood et al., 2019a). Indeed, engaging in any sort of bargaining is out of the question for many workers. This is not only because workers understand the futility of trying to bargain in the context of labour oversupply, but also because the digital architectures of platforms lend themselves to showing clients just how many workers are out there at any given time. As such, it is not uncommon to actually hear stories from workers about the ways in which they had to progressively reduce their rates over time. This happened to James who used his freelancing income to pay rent on an apartment in Nairobi. However, once his rates started going down because of market pressures, he could no longer afford to live there.

The global geography of workers serves to not just create enormous downwards pressure on wages through market forces, it also encourages workers to see themselves as competitors rather than colleagues. As such, when we asked online freelancers if they would ever consider being part of a trade union, the most frequent response we received was laughter. Factory workers or office workers have found much success in the past through the strategy of setting up picket lines. The spatial proximity inherent to pickets allows collective action by workers to grow in size and reduces the ability for workers to break ranks with one another. But for cloudworkers, there is no ability to use the spatial proximity deployed by those doing geographically tethered work. Workers in Ghana talk about Filipinos ready to do their jobs should they try to withdraw their labour, and Filipinos spoke of Indians willing to do their jobs for a fraction of the price. There's always a sense that someone else somewhere else will do the work for less money, and there's always a sense that the sort of solidarity needed to collectively withdraw labour is an impossibility. Cloudworkers therefore remain relatively atomized in how they interact with clients.

This atomization of cloudworkers, in turn, leads to a situation in which many workers have no choice but to accept whatever work they can find. The online freelancer in Ghana that we mentioned in the introductory chapter spoke of the multiple 48-hour stints that he went without sleep in order to deliver work on time for clients. The reason why he, and others like him, are willing to do this is because they are scared about getting anything other than a perfect five-star feedback score. In the context of an oversupply of labour power, workers know that they need to do everything in their power to avoid bad feedback. And almost every online freelancer has at least one story of an unsavoury client who realizes this and uses it as a threat should the worker not agree to extra hours, extra deliverables or lower rates.

4

How are workers reshaping the gig economy?

The aim of this chapter is not only to shine a spotlight on the new moments of resistance that gig work is creating, but also to understand that work is a phenomenon that always is shaped by both employers and workers – along with other preconditions that we discussed in chapter 1 like the role of the state and regulation. By examining how workers are resisting, organizing and shaping the gig economy, we can draw out different potential futures of work. However, when the gig economy and platform work was first recognized as a growing phenomenon around ten years ago, many commentators noted that traditional forms of worker representation would no longer be appropriate or adequate to protect these workers. The widespread use by platforms of self-employed independent contractor status not only creates the conditions of low pay and precarious work that we have discussed so far, but it also creates significant barriers to traditional forms of trade unionism.

Emerging forms of resistance in geographically tethered work

Geographically tethered work, as we have seen in previous chapters, shares many characteristics with the jobs that it has either replaced or displaced. When looking for examples of worker agency, some of these forms also share characteristics with more traditional forms of resistance. Worker resistance has historically covered a range of different activities, from the everyday activities of gossip, toleration and resignation, to the less common theft, sabotage and non-cooperation, as well as formal complaints and legal action (Tucker, 1993). The more open forms of collective action include strikes – the archetypal form of worker resistance (Hyman, 1989). The most effective forms of resistance come from the way the labour process is organized. For example, on assembly lines, workers found that they could shut down the line by only striking at particular points, using this to minimize lost pay. In new forms of work like digital labour, innovations are required to successfully organize, finding new weaknesses in the control of work (Woodcock, 2018b). There is therefore a learning process taking place in the gig economy, as workers find new and emerging forms of resistance and organization.

Worker resistance and organizing has historically drawn on the fact that workplaces tended to bring together groups of workers, put them in the same place for extended periods of time, and subject them to identical conditions. For example, factories were traditionally large workplaces, occupied by workers on shifts, working the same machines for the same pay. The time spent together meant that collective identities and grievances could form alongside the other social bonds that people make at work, providing a strong basis for collective action. The dispersed nature of platform work breaks down the possibilities of building networks and trust. For example, with Uber there is no reason why drivers need to spend time with each other. Compared to the minicab company with its shared garage and waiting area for drivers, there is no opportunity or reason for Uber drivers to meet. However, it is not the case that gig workers operate in a social vacuum – after all, the geographically tethered nature of the work means they work within the shared space of the city. This means sharing a workplace of sorts, albeit one much larger than a factory or office.

This meeting of workers can be seen clearly with the example of Deliveroo. Walking around many other European cities, Deliveroo workers are a common sight due to their bright turquoise bags and uniforms; similarly, the red of Zomato and orange of Swiggy across India, and the black and green of Uber Eats in New York City and the US. In some cases, the app directs drivers to a meeting point. This is an algorithmically determined location in each delivery zone, meant to ensure the driver is likely to be able to deliver the next order in the shortest possible time (Woodcock, forthcoming). From a computational perspective, this makes sense: analysing data and pushing for the greatest efficiency. From the workers' perspective, this means drivers finding themselves together in the same place. These become a stand-in for a more traditional workplace, providing the basis for the organizing that followed.

In 2016 in London, these meeting points became a focus for self-organization of Deliveroo workers. Workers met each other in these algorithmically determined meeting points, swapping numbers and starting WhatsApp groups (Waters and Woodcock, 2017). This led to the formation of overlapping networks that were used to share grievances, keep in contact and later build support for a strike (Woodcock, forthcoming). WhatsApp became an example of what Alex Wood (2015) has called 'mass self-communication networks'. As Kurt Vandaele (2018: 16) has noted more recently, these 'networks are serving as a "breeding ground" for self-organized courier associations boosting their associational power'. In June and July 2016, these networks clearly had a latent capacity for organizing in London. In August 2016, Deliveroo sent a message to drivers that it would be ending the hourly-rate payment scheme, moving instead to pay drivers per delivery. There was no option for workers to negotiate or discuss the changes. This left the workers with one option to voice their concerns about the changes: going on strike.

The UK, like many countries, has strict laws governing strike action. The issues of self-employment mean that in many contexts, workers cannot join a trade union – let alone have it recognized – or organize a legal strike. However, this also creates a kind of 'illusion of control' for platforms like Deliveroo (Woodcock, forthcoming). While they are able to use forms of 'algorithmic management' (Lee et al., 2015; Rosenblat and Stark, 2016; Rosenblat, 2018) to control the work, this becomes much harder when workers decide to resist. As Deliveroo riders were classified as self-employed, independent contractors, the regulations and laws governing strike action did not apply to them. If they choose not to log in for a shift, there was no way Deliveroo could challenge this, other than by discontinuing all of their contracts. This is an example of 'unauthorized walkouts – or the threat of them – the most dramatic of disruptive tactics' which previously have been 'a familiar and even routine part of grievance negotiations in such industries as coal mining, city transit, construction, automobile, steel, metalworking, and longshoring' (Kuhn, 1961: 50–1). Therefore, this first strike at a food delivery platform showed that 'stopping machines in the twentieth century corresponds to collective logouts in the twenty-first century' (Vandaele, 2018: 15). Strike action had not disappeared; instead, workers were in the process of mutating it into a new form.

From the starting point in London, these strikes spread across Europe in 2016 and 2017. As Callum Cant (2018) has argued, the 'official strike statistics do not sufficiently describe worker resistance in food platforms' as they don't capture this kind of action. Drawing on the same mass self-communication networks that were used to organize these strikes, Cant sourced reports of strikes from the UK, Netherlands, Germany, Spain, Belgium, France and Italy. Across the two years, he found '41 incidents across 18 months in 7 countries involving an estimated 1493 workers'. This led Cant to conclude that there are three features to food platform strikes: 'first is an increase in incidents over time. Second is a sporadic month by month but consistent quarterly increase in the total number of workers mobilized. Third is an increase in the synchronicity of mobilization across all seven countries.' This means that these strikes are not isolated occurrences, but rather part of a wave of struggles that are emerging in food delivery. There have since been strikes by Deliveroo workers in Hong Kong, as well as large strikes on other food delivery platforms in South Africa and India.

Across each of these incidents are the stories of workers delivering food without the employment protections they may have had previously. Each incident also has the stories of workers meeting each other, discussing, planning and then carrying out strikes – with no protection from mainstream trade unions. The strikes themselves have been creative, energetic and inspirational. What the strikes also show is that, despite the structural barriers to organizing, workers 'do have a certain workplace bargaining power'. As Vandaele (2018: 14) continues, workers' 'disruptive capacity stems from the delivery, transport and logistics system's key importance in the interaction between producers and customers'.

Following the strikes in 2016 in London, a section of the workers involved joined the IWGB. This is a small trade union that began organizing with mainly Latin American migrant workers in universities in London, but has now grown to represent couriers, Uber drivers, foster care workers, self-employed electricians and, most recently, videogame workers. The IWGB 'is a non-bureaucratic, grassroots, "bottom-up" organization'.[1] It is a registered union, but not affiliated to the TUC (Trade Union Congress). Outside of London, food delivery workers have joined the IWW (the Industrial Workers of the World), a radical union with a long history of organizing precarious workers (Fear, 2018). This model of grassroots trade unionism has been followed in different parts of Europe. For example, in Germany, riders have organized with FAU (Freie Arbeiter Union – Free Workers Union); with CLAP (Collectif des livreurs autonomes de Paris – Paris Autonomous Deliverers' Collective) in France; the Riders Union (FNV) in the Netherlands; and the Riders Union Padova and Riders Union Bologna in Italy, amongst others. These different groups are now coordinating across Europe through the Transnational Federation of Couriers. As one of the IWW members of the network explained: 'these companies operate on a transnational level, so we need to resist them on a transnational level.'[2]

Some of these struggles across Europe have evolved into protracted legal battles over the employment status of gig workers. The problem of self-employment status has made it difficult for workers to organize in traditional forms of trade unionism. As of 2018, the IWGB is engaged in two legal battles to overturn the self-employed independent contractor status at Deliveroo and Uber. The argument for doing so has been clearly articulated by Jason Moyer-Lee,[3] the general secretary of the IWGB. He points out that there are two sides in the public debate at present:

> [One side claims] the problem is confusion in the law, or the inability of the law to keep up with the times, which can result in workers being inadvertently deprived of rights to which they're entitled. On the other side of the debate, you have those of us who have been submitting and repeatedly winning tribunal cases establishing the 'gig economy's' labourers as limb (b) workers, in particular the Independent Workers' Union of Great Britain (IWGB), and of course the judges who are writing these decisions. We say the law is pretty clear and the companies are clearly on the wrong side of it.

Regardless of the decisions over employment status, workers are finding ways to resist and organize on platforms across the world. For example, when we were interviewing drivers in Bangalore, India, we would regularly hear stories of resistance. Every time we asked drivers (who worked for the largest food delivery platforms, Zomato and Swiggy, in Bangalore) if they were members of a union, they always answered 'no'. However, when we asked if they spoke to other workers about problems they had, we would hear stories of large WhatsApp groups of workers, or meeting places that workers would organize. In one stage of our fieldwork, we set off to find a meeting point for Zomato workers with our local research collaborators. After interviewing an autorickshaw driver (who now worked via the Uber app), he agreed to drive us to a popular meeting point in central Bangalore.

We were led to a row of restaurants with wide steps in front, as well as plenty of parking. Over the course of an hour, we sat on the steps discussing working conditions with a shifting group of around a dozen Zomato 'two-wheeler' (or motorcycle and moped) drivers. Some of them spoke to us the whole time, while others dropped in and out as the orders came in. The majority of the conversation was held in Kannada, with occasional English, and translated by our colleagues Pradyumna Taduri and Mounika Neerukonda. The drivers' zone had around 600 workers, delivering across a busy part of the city. When we discussed what they thought about their work, the replies centred around the falling piece-rate for deliveries. The workers explained they had set up WhatsApp groups and tried to complain to the platform, who did not respond to their grievances and refused to meet anyone claiming to be a representative of the drivers. As a result, the workers had recently gone on strike, with an estimated 400 workers taking part across their zone. The strike did not win any concessions, nor was it coordinated with any other delivery workers in the city. It is one glimpse of the bubbling resentment that platform workers were feeling, something that could otherwise be missed without talking to workers.

We heard similar stories in South Africa during our fieldwork. None of the drivers we spoke to were members of a trade union. There were, like the previous examples, large WhatsApp groups of workers, sharing experiences and grievances. In Cape Town we spoke to Ayanda, who worked for three different delivery platforms simultaneously. He explained how he would 'stack' orders, but always made sure to deliver the food before the packages, as 'the food has got to be warm by the time you deliver it!' While he said there were few problems with the package deliveries he made, there were more complaints with OrderIn for food delivery. Ayanda explained how the drivers formed a WhatsApp group to discuss what to do. He talked us through the example of a strike they had organized. The strike was pitched on the WhatsApp group and the majority of workers agreed. They then made sure to talk to other drivers they met on the street to prepare. When the strike day arrived, they all logged off from the app. We asked how they made sure that other drivers did not break the strike, tempted to 'boost' earnings from the platform. He replied that if other drivers went against the majority, 'we smashed up their bikes, that's democracy'. These tactics worked; the drivers had gone on strike multiple times over the last year, winning concessions from the platform each time. We asked whether they would form or join a union. Ayanda thought that there was no need to. He explained that there were no leaders, but they also did not need any: when they wanted to go on strike, they did. While we did not hear any other examples of strikes as widespread as on this platform, there were examples of smaller strikes and collective organizing across other platforms in South Africa.

Strikes in China show another example of workers finding new ways to resist and organize in a quite different context. In China there is technically only one union: the ACFTU (All-China Federation of Trade Unions), with around 303 million members. However, there is little opportunity for workers' autonomy as it is constitutionally subordinated to protecting national interests, does not hold elections, and is tied to the ruling party within a one-party state (Taylor and Li, 2007: 707). As has been argued by Bill Taylor and Qi Li (2007: 703–7), the ACFTU 'is not a legitimate trade union because it fails three tests of unionism'. First, its constitutional role includes protecting the 'national interest' not workers' interests; second, there is no election of officials by the rank-and-file membership; and third, the union is tied to the state ruling party within a one-party state, meaning there is little opportunity for workers' autonomy (Taylor and Li, 2007: 703–7). While the right to strike was removed in China in 1982, as noted by Taylor and Li, 'there is no legal prohibition on workers taking strike action'. This means that strikes operate in a grey area. Despite this, as the China Labour Bulletin has documented, there have been at least 10,000 strikes in China since 2011, including strikes of food delivery workers (China Labour Bulletin, 2018a). With grievances echoing those in Europe, Meituan workers struck across China because they were being 'paid less per delivery, penalized for not completing impossible orders, forced to risk their lives, sacked for talking about it' (China Labour Bulletin, 2018b).

While there have been strikes like these across the world, many of which have gone unreported, the UK was the starting point. In October 2018 these strikes changed in form again. Uber Eats riders went on strike against a change in payment terms that would reduce the amount they received per drop. Across the UK, riders had begun organizing with the IWW. They had success organizing riders outside of London, but following the spontaneous strikes on 20 October 2018, they called for a national strike to coincide with strikes at McDonald's, TGIFridays and Wetherspoons pubs in London, Cambridge and Brighton. This represented a significant shift in the organizing of food delivery platform workers, with coordinated strike action up the supply chain. There has also been organizing of Uber drivers, who in the UK formed the UPHD (United Private Hire Drivers), now a branch of the IWGB. While they coordinated with these other groups of workers, they also called their first ever strike in the UK on 9 October 2018 for 24 hours from 1pm. They demanded an increase of fares to £2 per mile, Uber to reduce commissions to 15 per cent, an end to unfair deactivations and bullying, and worker rights protection. As the branch chair, James Farrar argued:

> After years of watching take home pay plummet and with management bullying of workers on the rise, workers have been left with no choice but to take strike action. We ask the public to please support drivers by not crossing the digital picket line by not using the app during strike time. (IWGB, 2018)

This positioning of the app as a picket line represents a new way of understanding workplace struggle, re-pitching the picket line in more contemporary, digital terms.

It is not only Uber drivers in the UK who have started organizing against the platform. Across countries the kinds of resistance have differed, with action taken by existing taxi drivers against Uber in countries including across Europe, as well as Brazil, China, Indonesia and the US. However, this is not so much resistance by platform workers, but rather action against platforms (and therefore the workers who choose to work on them). While this kind of opposition has been incredibly widespread, there are emerging patterns of strikes by Uber drivers in different countries, including strikes in Bangladesh, India, Kenya, South Africa and the UK.

In India, there have been large strikes of Uber drivers, including drivers for Ola – the Indian-based competitor. For example, in October 2018 there was a combined strike of Uber and Ola drivers in Mumbai and Delhi, with demands for higher fares to meet rising fuel costs. These were coordinated by existing union organizations like the Mumbai Taxi Drivers' Union.[4] In Bangalore, we met with Tanveer Pasha, the President of Ola, Taxiforsure and Uber drivers and Owners Association, to discuss organizing at these companies. While there was little participation in Bangalore in the previous strike, the union represents around 55,000–60,000 drivers.[5] While they are yet to win concessions from Uber, it shows that sustained organization is possible.

The picture is complicated by the fact that Uber has been banned in a number of countries (while remaining to operate in some). Similarly, Uber has pulled out of China, leaving Didi Chuxing as the dominant company, while selling to Grab in Singapore and neighbouring Southeast Asian countries. In June 2018, drivers at Didi Chuxing went on strike across China. The action took different forms. For example, in Shaodong, Hunan, hundreds of workers were involved in a strike that lasted six days. They posted their grievances online, citing lost bonuses, high commission and long journeys for pickups. In Hangzhou, Zhejiang, workers were offered a new scheme that would provide a guaranteed income but required them to work for ten hours per day. Those drivers who did not join the scheme then started to receive less work, triggering the strike. The strikes were so large that transport workers accounted for 20 per cent of all workers on strike in China during that month (China Labour Bulletin, 2018c).

We have focused specifically on food delivery and taxi platform work, as this has seen the sharpest and most coordinated workers' action. However, only minor concessions have been admitted to by companies so far. For example, in 2017 riders working for Notime platform in Switzerland organized protests backed by the Unia union. They were successful, winning improvements to terms and conditions, as well as no longer being classed as independent contractors (Vandaele, 2018: 15).

There are also emerging stories of resistance on other kinds of platforms, many of which face significant barriers to organizing. For example, Juliet Schor[6] points out that on TaskRabbit, workers taking customers off-platform 'is very prevalent'. TaskRabbit allows customers to request location-specific tasks from workers, while charging a 20 per cent fee. Rather than continuing to have their pay docked by TaskRabbit, Schor notes that 'once the relationship with the client is established, they don't feel like TaskRabbit should take such a high fee.' The reliance on independent contractor or self-employed status makes the issue of worker retention difficult for platforms. To maintain the illusion of self-employed status, platforms cannot be seen to direct the work too closely or exert too much control. Otherwise workers can (successfully) challenge the status in court. This taking of work off-platform is a form of individual resistance. While not comparable to a collective strike, it points to the frustrations on the platform.

A story of how this kind of process can affect the platform can be found with the cleaning company Homejoy. At first the platform grew quickly, taking advantage of venture capital funding and aggressive discounts for customers. When Homejoy collapsed in 2015, the co-founder Adora Cheung claimed that the 'deciding factor' was the lawsuits brought by cleaners against the independent contractor status (Huet, 2015). However, much of the blame was also placed on how Homejoy acquired customers – particularly how the discounts were not converting into repeat customers – the model arguably did not work to keep workers on the platform. In fact, one former employee noted that 'maybe our retention was a lot better, but it was retention off the platform'.[7] For workers, it made sense to move off the platform after the introduction. After all, the platform took a significant cut of the cleaning fee, sometimes almost half. As one former worker explained, 'a lot of people who initially hired me through Homejoy have mentioned that they could hire me outside.' The platform charged $60 per hour, taking a cut of $25 per hour. Instead, the worker continued, 'when I work directly, I bill people at $40.'[8] This means that both the customer is saving money and the worker is making more. This process of work migrating off-platform was exacerbated by a failure of the platform to facilitate repeat relationships – the feature allowing a customer to hire the same worker again was only added just before the platform folded (Farr, 2015).

Cloudwork and resistance

As we have discussed with delivery and taxi work, some gig workers share the same workplace – even if that shared space is somewhere as diffuse as a city district. For cloudworkers, however, there are no necessary shared spaces of co-presence. With microwork, the labour process of each individual worker is fractured into many parts. Workers often do not know much about the purpose of the work that they are doing. Image taggers know that they are tagging images, but not why those images need to be tagged or who else is working on the project. Many workers have no idea how many others might be working on the same job or for the same client. This means that while they are often working as part of a group, they might never come into contact with other workers. This is no accident. Platforms are designed to facilitate some types of cooperation (for instance the negotiations between clients and workers) whilst limiting others (for instance providing any way for workers to identify or communicate with each other).

Online freelancing can also be deeply individualized. Many forms of freelance work are completed by a single worker in communication with the client. On the biggest platforms, freelancers only win contracts by bidding against other potential workers. This has an isolating tendency, setting workers against each other, rather than building bonds of solidarity over shared conditions. These factors lead to especially challenging barriers to organizing, as workers do not pass each other in the street, nor are they likely to live in the same neighbourhoods (even if they did, most wouldn't have any way of knowing). However, that is not to say that online freelancers are totally atomized. Many find and offer mutual support through forums, Facebook groups and other digital media. As Wood et al. (2018) have argued, 'internet-based communities enable workers to support each other and share information.

This, in turn, increases their security and protection. However, these communities are fragmented by nationality, occupation and platform.'

The risk here is that the technological innovations of this work are overemphasized, leading to a determinism that sees the ability of workers to resist and organize as already being defeated before they even start. As the previous section on geographically tethered work has demonstrated, resistance can – and does – take a wide range of forms. Resistance is taking place with cloudwork, but the emerging forms that it takes remain mostly below the surface. This does not mean that they are not important, but it can make them much harder to find – particularly for people who do not work those jobs. Even in the hardest conditions, workers are finding a voice in the gig economy. There have also been moments when this latent potential can be seen, showing how cloudwork could be reshaped in workers' interests.

Cloudworkers on Upwork, for instance, have developed ways to resist the surveillance methods forced upon them. On Upwork, screenshots are taken of the workers' computer screen at random intervals every ten minutes (this is only for work that is paid hourly rather than per task). In other words, the screenshot can be taken between second 0:01 and 10:00. If a client sees something unrelated to their job (say, the use of social media during work time), they can flag the image and the worker will not be paid for that ten-minute period. In response, workers have figured out two strategies to escape this surveillance. The first is setting up a second monitor and using that for games, social media and general internet browsing. The screenshot monitoring system only ever takes screenshots of the first screen – meaning they can do whatever they want on the second screen. Second, if a screenshot happens early enough into the ten-minute slot (e.g. at minute 5), the worker knows that they have five minutes before another screenshot is going to be taken. Some use this to not work on the client's job. These tactics are only used by a minority of workers, as many freelancers have internalized a need to be efficient for their clients and consider this sort of strategy to be unethical. However, the existence of these sorts of practices show that cloudwork is not as efficient and as free of resistance as it might at first appear. Even in the most controlled of environments, workers are able to push back against their labour being treated as a commodity.

One of the most powerful examples of the ability for workers to resist and organize comes from an intervention made on the Amazon Mechanical Turk platform. Workers in Mechanical Turk, and similar platforms, face a host of challenges: the disciplinary use of ratings, the prevalence of non-payment for work and the lack of communication channels for workers. As a response, the Turkopticon project was developed by Lilly Irani and Six Silberman. It is 'an activist system that allows workers to publicize and evaluate their relationships with employers. As a common infrastructure, Turkopticon also enables workers to engage one another in mutual aid' (Irani and Silberman, 2013: 611). Turkopticon provides a browser plug-in that produces an overlay for workers while they are on the platform. It allows workers to share their rating of the requester – thus reversing the Panopticon-like relationship between platform and workers[9] – to try and hold employers accountable for their treatment. Turkopticon then included a forum through which workers could meet and discuss online.

The importance of Turkopticon is that it shows workers can collectively organize on the platform. Although it began as an outside intervention, the design promotes workers' self-activity through its use. Rather than workers being organized from outside, it provides a way for workers to begin to organize themselves. In this way, it is an embryo of new forms of digital worker organization, subverting the tools that are used in the work process and finding new uses for them. This was later iterated with the 'Dynamo' platform that aimed to 'support the Mechanical Turk community in forming publics around issues and then mobilizing' (Salehi et al., 2015). One part of this was the letter-writing campaign, which we discussed earlier in the book, which drew attention to the working conditions on the platform (Dynamo, 2014).

What Turkopticon also provides is a way for workers to come into contact with each other. It shows that, despite not needing to share the same geographical location to complete the work, workers can still collaborate. Like the Deliveroo workers who share the same streets and hang around by the restaurants, microworkers too share the same communication channels and hang around on forums. Digital communication is a key part of this work (Gupta et al., 2014; Gray et al., 2016), and forums have been shown to be important (Yin et al., 2016). The forum acts as a place for workers to share tips and grievances, operating in a similar way to the WhatsApp groups. For the cloudworker, the forum is the equivalent of the street corner for the geographically tethered worker, which is broadly equivalent to the gates at the dock for the prospective docker. Clearly there are differences between these three meeting points. The forum lacks material co-presence, building comparatively weaker connections. The street corner may bring platform workers together, but only at that corner, and not across the whole city. The gates of the dock bring together a critical mass of workers. However, the dock gate was also not the perfect environment to organize – after all, workers are competing against each other to be 'called on' (whether directly or indirectly). Nevertheless, each is a location in which workers can potentially meet and start collectively organizing for better conditions. In online work this is becoming widespread. A survey by Wood et al. (2018: 100–1), for instance, showed that 58 per cent of cloud-workers in their sample communicated with other online workers at least once a week, either through social media, SMS, email or on forums. Communication is an important first step towards collective resistance and organizing.

Towards a new kind of trade unionism?

The evidence so far is that workers on geographically tethered platforms the world over are increasingly fighting to reshape platform work. There are visible – as well as more hidden – examples of strikes and organizing now spreading across the planet. Even at this early stage, there have been some limited successes for those workers. While the struggles of cloudworkers to reshape and control parts of their work also remain at a nascent stage, there is emerging evidence that worker resistance is also present in – what on the surface – appears to be highly controlled and atomized worker processes. At this point it is important to remember that while cloudwork is new, it builds upon histories of other kinds of precarious work – indeed, cloudworkers may already have experienced precarious work, and perhaps developed tactics to deal with it.

This resistance is happening within structurally difficult conditions, often in grey areas of legality, or even taking place illegally. This is because, in many locales, the self-employed are not allowed to form trade unions like workers or employees are. In those places, doing so is seen as operating like a price-setting cartel rather than simply providing a means for workers to bargain over their pay. In fact, the US Chamber of Commerce, of which Uber and Lyft are members, has argued in a Seattle court that 'by allowing drivers to bargain over their pay, which is based on fares received from passengers, the city would permit them to essentially fix prices in violation of federal antitrust law.'[10] This measure has been seen as an attempt to prevent the Teamsters from organizing Uber drivers in Seattle.

The threats of legal injunctions mean that workers are not only having an effect on the gig economy, but are redefining what organizing and trade unionism mean today. It is worth noting here that the kinds of trade unions that exist today have come quite far from the early forms of unions. The struggles of textile workers have been traced as far back as 1675, then later linked with Luddism and the smashing of machinery in England, but their actions can also be read as a response to their economic conditions, rather than just an opposition to machinery per se (Binfield, 2004). Many textile workers participated in the demonstration in Manchester in 1819 calling for parliamentary reform – now infamous as the Peterloo Massacre, after cavalry charged the protestors, killing 15 people and injuring hundreds more. In 1833, six agricultural labourers swore a secret oath to join The Friendly Society of Agricultural Labourers in the Dorset village of Tolpuddle, with the aim of protesting their falling wages. After their discovery, they were sentenced to penal transportation to Australia, becoming famous as the Tolpuddle

Martyrs (Marlow, 1971). It took until 1871 for trade unions to be fully legalized in the UK, less than twenty years before the struggles of the London dock workers that we discussed in chapter 1.

It is important to remember, therefore, that many attempts by workers to organize activities start out neither as legally allowed nor institutionally accepted. Organizing in groups, formal trade unions, collective bargaining, strikes, picketing, and so on all began as illegal activities. It was only through the success of these tactics and the collective strength of workers that they became legitimized (at least in part). Even now, many of these activities are highly regulated or even prevented in some sectors (such as the armed forces or other areas deemed important to national security). In the UK, for example, workers cannot simply decide to go on strike for any reason. The strike must be a 'trade dispute' related to terms and conditions, and cannot be 'secondary action' in support of other workers. A postal ballot has to be organized among the union members, overseen by an independent party, and the employers informed. The ballot then must return a majority in favour, and the turnout among the members is required be over 50 per cent. The results need to be announced and the employer can apply for a court injunction to prevent the strike. If it goes ahead, the employer must be informed at least seven days beforehand. While this may then allow a legal strike to go ahead, the bounds within which such action can be taken are relatively narrow.

It is important to note that there is much more to workplace struggle than legally sanctioned industrial action, and indeed we have identified a range of different forms of worker resistance throughout this chapter, including forming of networks, unofficial strikes and protests. The vast majority of these do not have the support of legal trade unions – IWGB and other alternative unions in Europe are the exception here – and are often technically illegal. And we should also note that networks of workers or smaller unions have far fewer resources than larger official trade unions. This means that while there may be exciting developments at the workplace level (however we define that in the context of the gig economy), these remain on a relatively small scale, and isolated from the wider workers movement.

This isolation can be explained in two ways. First, many unions are simply not trying to organize with these workers. Although mainstream trade unions would not admit this publicly, one UK organizer has observed to one of the authors that it was not possible to organize drivers, because: 'how would you even find them?' Without wanting to castigate that particular union, it is not beyond the stretch of imagination to actually use the platform to place an order to come into contact with a worker. What this highlights is that some older unions appear to be unwilling to organize these new groups of workers. From an organizational perspective, this makes sense. Gig economy workers are far less likely than workers in traditional waged employment to pay consistent dues to the union, meaning that recruitment is not a solution to the ongoing crisis of membership and funding that many unions face (or will face in the near future). Most mainstream unions also simply do not have the 'boots-on-the-ground' understanding needed to organize with gig workers. Successful organizing of these highly distributed workers takes time, commitment and resources. If there is an expectation of a quick return on investment through union dues, organizing in the gig economy does not make immediate sense – an outcome that leads many to argue that gig workers are unorganizable.

These kinds of arguments have been made, and proven wrong, before. For example, workers in the car industry in the early twentieth century, as well as those 'working seasonally across a range of industries' were 'regarded as unorganizable' (McIlroy, 1995: 9). However, during the Second World War, car factories became a focus of organizing, with strength continuing to build afterwards. The car industry became a bastion of trade unions in the UK (Beynon, 1973), until their decline with changes after the 1970s, with the greater use of technology and fewer jobs as much of the production moved overseas.

The work we have discussed so far is clearly very different to the car industry. However, it is still work, and work still involves the buying and selling of people's time. This creates a tension between the buyer and seller, particularly when the seller pushes to drive down the costs of their 'self-employed' workforce. What we have tried to draw attention to is the activity of workers trying to change their conditions in various ways. While on a surface level there may not be widespread organized resistance, the same process that Harry Braverman (1998) identified in factory work can be found too:

> But beneath this apparent habituation, the hostility of workers to degenerated forms of work which are forced upon them continues as a subterranean stream that makes its way to the surface when the conditions permit, or when the capitalist driver for a greater intensity of labour oversteps the bound of physical or mental capacity. It renews itself in new generations, expresses itself in the unbounded cynicism and revulsion which large number of workers feel about their work, and comes to the fore repeatedly as a social issue demanding a solution.

This is not to say that we are on an inevitable march towards effective resistance and organization of workers, but rather that this work still contains tensions between employers and workers (however defined) and that both sides will push to get a better deal from the relationship. No matter how work is organized, workers will always have power. As Kim Moody (2017: 69) has noted 'a new terrain of class struggle has emerged' beyond the gig economy, 'which in many ways is more favorable to working-class initiatives'. The trick is figuring out how it can best be harnessed in our new world of work.

Conclusion:
What next for the gig economy?

The gig economy is not just a synonym for algorithmic wizardry, large datasets and cutting-edge technologies. Whenever we think (or indeed research or write) about work, it is important to remember that work necessarily involves workers. This means actual people with complex lives, working in relationships with each other.

When talking about the numbers of workers in the gig economy across the world, the everyday lived experiences of these workers can fade into the background. After all, with millions of stories, we cannot possibly as individuals relate to all of them. However, when thinking at the macro scale of millions of workers, it is more than just individual stories or experiences that are harder to grasp. When workers become numbers that are graphed or plotted, their agency – whether collective or individual – fades into the background. The gig economy thereby risks being understood as something that is done to workers, rather than something they engage with, create and produce, in different ways.

While we still need a macro-level analysis and mappings of the gig economy, that sort of work needs to be combined with stories about workers' own experiences, both as a redress to the anonymizing character of platforms, and to centre their voices in any proposed changes. Furthermore, many of the stories that we hear about the gig economy – from the budding entrepreneur on Upwork in the slums of Nairobi to the single mother in Nebraska taking advantage of the scheduling flexibility that Uber affords her – only paint part of the picture. If the gig economy is coming to define ever more of the economy, it is not good enough to focus just on those who thrive in it. Such feel-good stories, so often shared in the media by the PR arms of platforms, policymakers who don't have the sense to know better, and academics who have been bought off with privileged access to proprietary platform data, distract from the real winners in changes to labour markets that shift risk in one direction and reward in the other. The gig economy is built by design to convenience consumers, to return profit to platforms and, ultimately, to disempower workers. We therefore need a concerted effort to understand the cracks that many fall through. We need to focus on those that are excluded, those that are disadvantaged, and the ultimate winners and losers in what has become a profound reorganization of how many people work.

Workers are never passive participants in work. They bring with them a range of experiences, expectations, relationships and desires to work. While the role of management is to try and control work, workers too can reshape it. Work is therefore a site of constant contestation between the different interests of workers, managers and owners. As we have shown in chapter 4, it should therefore come as no surprise that there is significant resistance in the gig economy. Too often we consider resistance to just involve trade unions and strike action, but the reality is that resistance takes place across a wide spectrum of actions.

Anyone who claims that there is no worker agency or resistance in the gig economy is simply not looking in the right place. That resistance may take many forms, including the delivery drivers complaining about work outside a restaurant, the spreading of WhatsApp groups, joining trade unions, burning tyres and vandalizing bikes during wildcat strikes, sharing scripts that automate menial tasks, and other new forms of organization that are only just beginning to emerge. What the examples of resistance show is that the gig economy is already being contested every day across the world. What is less clear, however, is how that contestation will be resolved, and whose interests will be benefitted.

The gig economy that we know today only exists because of the digital transformation that we are in the midst of. Mass connectivity, the almost ubiquitous availability of phones and computers, the digital legibility of work, the pressure from an economically globalized world combined with outsourcing, and the emergence of platforms that harness vast databases to match supply and demand for labour power have ushered in a world of work that represents a departure from older ways of organizing the labour process.

But today's gig economy is not just enabled by technology. Particular political and social circumstances – consumer attitudes and preferences, gendered and racialized relationships of work, permissive regulatory environments, ineffective trade union resistance, and a general desire for flexibility from both employers and workers – have also allowed for employment relationships in which workers are atomized units competing for jobs in open markets. Within the economic transformation within which we find ourselves, work is becoming temporary, unstable, mediated, patchworked and persistently contestable (Peck, 2017). This is happening across sectors and around the world as a result of particular technological, social, political and economic preconditions.

Work, for those in the gig economy, is on demand, no longer embedded in organizations, and mediated by platforms that capture significant rents. It is often characterized by informational opacity and asymmetry, with workers knowing little about the production networks that they are embedded into. It is an individualized pursuit with few opportunities to build a stable cohort of colleagues. It is becoming ephemeral, with today's work not necessarily resembling yesterday's. It is highly fragmented, with some jobs measured in minutes or even seconds rather than months or years. It is relatively unregulated and tends to evade much labour law through a re-classification of the relationship between the employer and worker. And it is almost always defined by a relationship in which the burden of training and risk is put onto the worker rather than the client, the platform or the state. Workers who become injured, need time off for caring duties, or want to save up for retirement need to make sure that they have planned appropriately. Where once it might have been unthinkable – and certainly unfeasible – to have entire industries defined by contingent work, it now seems increasingly possible to Uberize yet another profession.

What is important to note here is that most workers in the gig economy actually want a level of flexibility. We have spoken to workers who talk emphatically about how platforms allow them to work in ways that would simply not otherwise have been possible; whether this means escaping some of the constraints of the local labour market, or doing jobs they would not have been able to access previously. These people like the anonymity, they like the flexibility, and they are happy with the pay.

Indeed, gig economy firms like Uber and Deliveroo waste no time in sharing case studies of happy workers when faced with demands to improve working conditions. They remind workers that the last thing they want are nine-to-five jobs on traditional employment contracts in which they lose the ability to control their schedules. In many of the international-level policy meetings we have attended, the response from the well-dressed men sent to represent the interests of those platforms is usually to revert to anecdote – for example, about the single mother who needs the flexibility afforded by platform work to schedule jobs around her caring duties. Here they are careful to frame platform work not as something that her livelihood depends on (otherwise we might want to subject the relationship to a bit more scrutiny), but rather as a means for her to earn a bit of extra income in a relaxed way. Indeed, in many of those same meetings, when we speak about our own research with gig workers, one of the first comments from the platform representatives tends to be: 'these people aren't workers'. We need to have this discussion outside of these discursive boundaries. As we argued earlier in the book, these are workers. And these sorts of responses are just part of a fantastically powerful public relations machine that is reshaping how we think of work – by framing it as anything but work.

This is obviously only one part of the story. The dependence of workers on platform jobs varies by job type, but we do know that across sectors significant numbers of people rely on platforms for their livelihoods. While we have spoken to gig workers in India and South Africa who regularly work over twelve hours a day, seven days a week, evidence is increasingly showing that it is becoming harder to work full-time as incomes fall. We also have to ask ourselves who ultimately benefits from these arrangements. We should be asking not just whether workers like their jobs, but rather what are the political, economic, technological and social preconditions that have brought these activities into being, and whether those enablers ultimately mean that ever more jobs will fall under the shadow of the gig economy.

It is also worth noting that the sorts of conversations mentioned above about the virtues of platform work tend to be with people who have found ways of succeeding in their corner of the gig economy. And they are conversations with people who have not yet fallen upon misfortune as most of us do at some point in our lives. People in the prime of their lives who have a flexible job are, of course, going to value those jobs. What we have to ask ourselves is whether we would hear the same stories from the workers who tried and never made it onto the cloud platforms because of the lack of jobs?; would we hear the same stories from the Uber drivers accused of something by customers and deactivated from the platform with no due process; would we hear the same stories from food delivery riders who suffer an injury and have to go two months without pay until they can ride a bike again? The gig economy represents a way of organizing work in which the strong and the able can thrive, but in which the weak can fall through the cracks. It is all of our responsibility to remember who the gig economy does not work for, and why it does not work for them, when thinking about the benefits that it offers to workers.

Do we want a society in which long-term employment contracts are increasingly a thing of the past and in which ever more work is mediated by platform intermediaries? Do we want to shift even more risk onto workers? Do we all really want to trade our job security for flexibility – and the precarity that often follows? Few would disagree that flexible contracts are needed in some instances and some sectors. But how many jobs in the economy should actually be defined by gigs?

In this book we have shown how the gig economy involves an organizational form that is beginning to characterize ever more sectors of the economy. We have done this through a focus on a range of activities in a range of places. The gig economy is not just an extension of previous forms of labour market precarity. It is a reshaping of the spatialities and temporalities of work through particular enablers.

The Fordism of the assembly line changed the place and time of work, seeking to treat workers like machines, transforming not only the factory, but society more broadly. Now the gig economy is changing the places and times of work too. The economic geographies and temporalities of the gig economy make it challenging for workers to build effective and lasting structural power, hinder the ability of regulators to apply labour law, entrench the monopoly power of platforms as key intermediaries between supply and demand of labour, and ultimately bring about high levels of opacity that prevent the various actors in production networks from holding each other accountable. Unlike the Fordist era, today's workers are expected to be not machines, but rather entrepreneurs and atomized individuals. Although it may not be apparent at first glance, today's gig economy workers are also part of a bigger machine, albeit one held together by fibre optics, databases and algorithms.

Rather than accept that this is just how the machine works, we want to try to envision some alternative mechanics. We have done this framed around four problematic characteristics of the gig economy: a lack of transparency, accountability, worker power and democratic ownership. In some cases, we propose tweaks to the machine; in others we propose a fundamental rebuilding; and in yet others, we are simply suggesting places in which spanners might be effectively inserted to stop the cogs. For each of the four issues in this conclusion, we tried to rethink the political, economic, technological and social reconfigurations that would be needed to bring into being alternative and fairer futures for the workers of the gig economy. In all cases, we see each of the four futures as inherently intertwined. Each of them supports each other. And each of them is less effective when considered in isolation.

If we acknowledge that today's gig economy is not just a natural and inevitable outcome of technological changes, and instead is a particular mode of organization that was nurtured and brought into being by specific human and organizational actors with specific vested interests, then we can also acknowledge that alternative outcomes are possible. There is not enough space here for a full exposition or a detailed roadmap of any of these paths. We hope merely to expose the beginnings of a range of strategies and ideas; and by focusing on these four issues, their preconditions and enablers, and then four alternative futures, we can see that the undesirable aspects of today's gig economy are neither inevitable nor irrevocably locked in. We can no longer turn back the clock to some idealized past. But, by reflecting on the nature of gig work, we can still shape its futures.

Future #1: Transparency

Many of the problematic production practices in the gig economy are shielded by the opacity that is present within almost all digital production networks. Users, clients and consumers often know little about what is behind the screen or the app. This opacity is articulated in Susskind's (2018) piece on 'outcome thinking'. He argues that we should all be interested in the outcomes that workers bring, rather than the outcome of work on workers: 'clients don't really want us. They want the outcomes we bring', he notes. Indeed, most platforms encourage this state of affairs. When you use a platform to outsource a task, order food or even contract with a house cleaner, you are not encouraged to build long-term bonds with workers. They are instead presented as largely interchangeable beings in the market for talent. The entire model of most platforms in not premised on connecting clients to the perfect worker for them, but rather on indicating that clients and consumers have choice from a vast pool of workers.

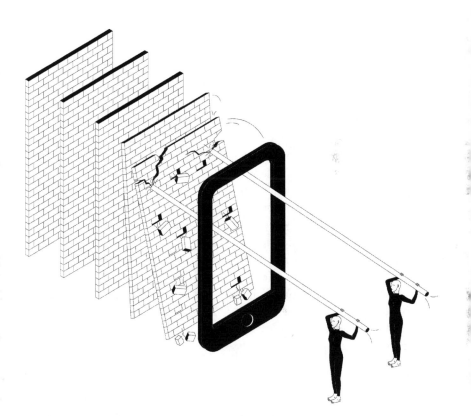

Figure 5 Transparency
Illustration by John Philip Sage

This de-personalization (and some might say de-humanization) of workers is not the norm in non-platform gig work around the world. In Britain, it is common to invite tradespeople in for a cup of tea and a chat about the weather or the football before they get down to work. In Kenya, it is not uncommon for people to pay for school fees or medical costs for the families of cleaners or gardeners that service their homes. Everywhere else in the world, we altruistically share time, stories, food and drink, advice and resources with the myriad workers that we encounter on a daily basis. We do this because of our social nature: feeling empathy, concern and care for people we barely know.

The efficiencies of platform services deprive us of much of that. Our relationships with workers are turned into a simple ranking and reputation system designed to regulate the performance of workers (Gandini, 2016). As we strip away the possibilities for social bonds and empathy, users, consumers and clients have few opportunities to get to know about the working conditions that define what it is like to work in the gig economy. We know little about whether workers enjoy their jobs, how precarious their income is, how vulnerable they are to change, whether they are paid a living wage, or whether they face discrimination or dangerous working conditions. The gig economy, in short, is defined by opacity and alienation.

But it need not be that way. We agree with Susskind that clients want outcomes. However, they also want more than that. How many of us would knowingly support companies that we know are actively engaging in destructive production practices? Indeed, a central reason why large companies spend so much money on corporate social responsibility is to ensure that they are not perceived as unethical. This desire for companies to be seen to be doing the right thing in order to avoid the reputational damage that could come with bad press has sparked an immense range of kitemarks, schemes and standards, all with the intent of informing consumers that the commodities that they buy are produced in ethically sensitive ways. There is always a danger here that such schemes can simply de-link the relationships between consumerism, capitalist production and global poverty (Cook, 2004; Richey and Ponte, 2011).[1] However, on the whole, it appears undeniable that individuals and businesses are more concerned than ever about what lies on the other side of the supply chains that they embed themselves into as consumers.

This brings us to our first future. We think there is a need for more transparency in the production networks of platform work, precisely in order to re-link capitalist production practices and poverty in the minds of consumers. In other words, we need a movement to help users, consumers, clients and platforms perceive the moral responsibility that they have for the livelihoods of workers. The first step here is to demystify the production process, and to build mechanisms so that platforms can no longer conceal what happens behind the app.

Platform companies may well fear the consequences of greater transparency in their production networks. It is worth remembering Tom Goodwin's now famous observation of the platform economy: 'Uber, the world's largest taxi company, owns no vehicles. Facebook, the world's most popular media owner, creates no content. Alibaba, the most valuable retailer, has no inventory. And Airbnb, the world's largest accommodation provider, owns no real estate.'[2] These companies, in other words, rely solely on their ability to control flows of information and act as intermediaries between clients and workers. If Uber and Upwork were to collapse tomorrow, the drivers, cars, computers and customers previously enrolled into their platform would still exist.

The move to deny platforms total control over information flows between suppliers and consumers can be achieved in a number of ways. The first is through research. Here we need to go beyond the numbers. It is not enough to simply scrape, map and model the economics of large platforms. We instead need to recall Marx's (1845) famous '11th thesis', that while 'philosophers have hitherto only interpreted the world in various ways; the point is to change it.' Inspired by that mission, and examples of action research in the gig economy (e.g. Irani, 2013; van Doorn, 2018), we have begun a broad-reaching research project to address issues of opacity in the gig economy.

The Fairwork project is a response that we developed to address many of the challenges that platform workers face across the world. The core mission of the project is to give a rating to every gig work platform that reflects the fairness of working conditions on the platform. The project began in early 2018 with a grant from Germany's Federal Ministry for Economic Cooperation and Development, and the convening of a large meeting at the International Labour Organization in Geneva to which we invited a diverse group of workers, trade unions, platforms, policy makers and academics. In that meeting, and follow-ups in Johannesburg and Bangalore, we were able to establish a set of five principles for 'fair work' in the gig economy. The principles cover fair pay (paying at least a minimum wage in the worker's jurisdiction), fair conditions (protecting worker health and well-being), fair contracts (at a minimum following national law and having a clear contract, and not engaging in the misclassification of workers), fair governance (having an appeals process for disciplinary procedures, and policies that ensure equality in the ways workers are managed), and finally, fair representation (having a process through which worker voice can be expressed, and recognizing collective bodies like unions where they exist). These five principles are converted into a possible score of ten for each platform. This involves two points for each principle, the first for achieving a basic level of fairness (for example, reaching a minimum level of fair pay), which if achieved, can result in a further point for a higher level of fairness (for example, guaranteeing a higher level of fair pay).

Through the ratings that are being produced through the project and put into an annual league table, a degree of transparency will be infused into the gig economy. Platforms and clients will no longer be able to hide behind the veil of the app, and instead can be held accountable by consumers. By utilizing the same rating scheme for all platforms, and allowing best (as well as worst) practices to be highlighted, it lessens the opportunities for anyone to shrug away problems with the statement that 'that couldn't work for our business model'. We do not see this as a panacea for the gig economy. Rather, it is a way to take inspiration from progressive organizations like the Living Wage Foundation in order to establish a clear set of fair work principles for the gig economy which could ultimately be used not just by platforms and clients, but also by workers: as benchmarks to embed into future campaigns and bargaining with platforms.

The second strategy through which platforms can be made more transparent is through the establishment of 'counter' platforms that seek to allow workers a degree of control. This involves countering the level of informational control that existing platforms have over the activities that they mediate. We have already discussed Turkopticon as an example of a counter platform, and will revisit the example in 'Future #3' below. But there are many other examples of hubs for platform workers to engage in collaborative information sharing and horizontal communication outside of the walls of the platforms that they work for. The Fair Crowd Work website (http://faircrowd.work/) run by Germany's largest trade union, IG Metall,[3] Sweden's white-collar union, Unionen, and the Austrian Chamber of Labour, is a platform that allows workers to rate platforms using a five-star rating system (mirroring the ways that workers get rated on most platforms). However, by far the most used counter platforms by workers are groups that workers set up on commonly used platforms like Facebook, WhatsApp and reddit. On those groups, workers are no longer constrained by the limited affordances that platforms seek to create for horizontal communication amongst workers, and they are no longer constrained by the limitations on the types of information that platforms allow workers to post about their jobs, their clients, their pay or anything else (also discussed in more detail in 'Future #3'). Workers, in other words, are finding ways to share the information that they want to share about the ways in which their jobs work.

We have seen how the opacity of digital production networks can allow for problematic upstream outcomes. If clients and consumers know little about working conditions, there is an incentive to cut costs to the end user at the expense of the wages and job conditions of workers. Yet by making work practices more visible, a combination of human empathy on the side of consumers, the reputational fears of firms, and the demystification of work processes that can help to develop shared worker consciousness about their jobs, can be harnessed to bring about fairer futures in the gig economy. It is undeniable that many people enact 'outcome thinking' in how they approach the world. Yet, there are probably at least as many who embed an ethic of care and empathy in how they interact with others. This is not a simple argument that somehow ethical consumption decisions can fix everything that is wrong with platform capitalism. They cannot and they will not. We are not all equally responsible for the problems baked into the gig economy, and we do not have equal power to change those problems. But, together, we can impose change by insisting on knowing more about the impacts of our actions. Building mutual understanding about work and working conditions is a starting point for larger structural change. Narratives about what the gig economy is need to be taken away from its current gatekeepers. By building more transparency about the nature of platform work, workers and their advocates lay the foundations for a more just world of work.

Future #2: Accountability

Our first future is about trying to better understand the networks that platforms mediate – from sites of work to sites of consumption, and everything in between. The lack of publicly available knowledge about how platforms work has meant that, in most parts of the world, they are faced with very little accountability. From Lagos to London to Los Angeles, platforms are making the case that they are a new, special type of technology firm. 'We're a technology company, not a taxi service, says Uber', reads the headline of a South African newspaper reporting an interview with a company spokesperson.[4] Uber's argument, made at an employment tribunal in London in 2016, is that it is a technology company because instead of providing a transport service to customers, 'it merely puts them in touch with drivers'.[5] In response to this, the following quote was heard during the *O'Connor vs Uber Technologies Inc.* case in the US in 2015:

Figure 6 Accountability
Illustration by John Philip Sage

Uber does not simply sell software; it sells rides. Uber is no more a 'technology company' than a Yellow Cab is a 'technology company' because it uses CB radios to dispatch taxi cabs.

To which the judge responded: 'we respectfully agree'.[6]

Despite this, platform companies deploy this kind of framing to argue that they have little responsibility to the millions of workers who rely on them for a daily income. If you, as a worker, want to take a holiday or need to take sick leave, the 'technology company' that simply connected you to your clients certainly is not going to help you out. But platforms are no more just technology companies than a shop or a factory is just a building. Platforms reap huge rewards from the positions they occupy as infomediaries, and so it does not seem unreasonable to expect them to shoulder a certain amount of accountability and responsibility for the lives of the workers that fuel their businesses.

The issue is that most platform managers are not just going to wake up one day and miraculously decide to become more responsible, putting at risk delivering profit to shareholders. Platforms can use regulation that was not designed with the platform economy in mind in order to have the best of both worlds: rewards without risk and responsibility.

Our first step here is therefore a discursive one. We need to stop imagining that platforms inhabit some sort of separate 'technological' realm of society. Taxi companies, cleaning companies, delivery companies and outsourcing companies are, and have always been, companies that use technology. For platform companies to now fetishize the information and communication technologies that power their business is clearly a strategic and self-serving move. Yes, platforms use technology. But no, they are not technology companies. They are transport companies, delivery companies and employment agencies, and so on. We need to start talking about them in that way.

Despite the efforts of platform lobbyists arguing that ministries of labour are against progress or that outdated labour laws no longer work, there has been a range of successes in trying to regulate platform work. Much effort has been expended here to get limited protection for workers via the courts, by arguing that gig workers are employees and that they therefore deserve the protections traditionally afforded to employees. For instance, a Valencia court, in June 2018, noted that Deliveroo riders are employees because they are 'subject to tight control by the platform monitoring their delivery rides, with GPS features, and to the laying down of the main terms and conditions, including prices' (Aloisi, 2018). Control is considered to be a key index of employment status. Those riders will therefore have all of the rights that employees are entitled to under Spanish law. In Australia, a Foodora food delivery worker was reclassified as an employee by the country's Fair Work Commission who noted that the platform 'had considerable capacity to control the manner in which the applicant performed work, and it fixed the place of work and the start and finish times of each engagement or shift' (see De Stefano 2018).[7] At The Doctors Laboratory in London, the IWGB won a union recognition agreement, with a range of employment statuses for riders previously part of a gig economy set-up (from full employee through to worker and self-employed). The benefits of this include representation, secure wages and increased bargaining power management.[8]

As these examples demonstrate, turning to the courts can be a useful means to secure protection for gig economy workers – at least those who have succeeded. Unfortunately, for most, this is ultimately a losing battle (Aloisi, 2018). Today's victory can quickly turn into tomorrow's loss, should the platform companies decide to tweak their policies to ensure that the next court decision deems platform workers are not entitled to the rights and protections of employees after all.

Even more troubling is the fact that some platform companies even seek to evade the rules that clearly do apply to them. Uber's South African entity (Uber Technologies SA) was recently taken to the Commission for Conciliation, Mediation and Arbitration (CCMA) by a trade union on behalf of some Uber drivers who were 'deactivated' from the platform.[9] The union demanded that Uber Technologies recognize drivers as employees and so give workers the protections afforded to employees under South African labour law. Uber appealed the decision at the Labour Court. The court decided that the case could not proceed – not because it had no merit, but rather because the claim was made against the wrong Uber entity. It turns out that Uber International Holding(s) BV, a company based in the Netherlands, owns the Uber software application, and, as such, all South African drivers are in a contract with Uber BV rather than Uber SA. South African Uber drivers would therefore have to take up their case in a court in the Netherlands.

There is no predestined reason why Uber drivers in South Africa should have a contract with the Dutch parent company rather than the local company. But the way Uber has structured the relationship is that Uber BV controls the drivers in South Africa and Uber Technologies SA provides support services to the drivers (for instance recruitment and onboarding) (du Toit, 2018). This use of multiple jurisdictions in order to operate a taxi company with an app is simply a way of ensuring that there is even more of an arm's-length relationship between the company and its workers.[10]

These decisions mean that, in order to hold platforms truly accountable through the courts and regulation, changes are needed. The first step is supporting workers and their advocates who have taken the fight to the courts. The second is identifying the cross-cutting needs and conditions of platform workers across sectors in order for broad protections to be brought into being. For instance, the South African Labour Relations Act and the Australian Independent Contractors Act both go some way to extending rights to all platform workers, irrespective of their employment status. We also need to look beyond existing labour law that, in most places, was designed for white-collar workers in offices and blue-collar workers in factories. In many places, the law simply is not designed to meet the needs of gig workers. If the platform as an intermediating party between clients or customers and workers is here to stay, and if we acknowledge that there are some cases in which the relationship between workers and platform looks substantially different to a traditional employment relationship, we then require protections that are either tailored to platform workers or exist independent of employment status.

Across Europe, both workers and unions have fought in the courtrooms to clarify employment status – either as employees, or in the UK with the application of 'worker status', in order to gain employment rights and protections. Although there have been test cases, Countouris and De Stefano (2019: 57) have argued that 'This relative quiet at a national policy level can be usefully contrasted with the more lively debate currently taking place at the EU level particularly around the draft Directive on Transparent and Predictable Working Conditions in the European Union.' This has the potential to extend rights, as Countouris and De Stefano (as well as the European Trade Union Confederation, ETUC) note that its stated aim is 'to provide protection for the widest categories of workers and in particular the most vulnerable workers'.

In the UK, the government commissioned a major report into the realities and futures of contemporary work. The results were published in *The Taylor Review of Modern Working Practices* (2017), with Matthew Taylor as the lead author. While the report itself has some critical internal issues – for example, Greg Marsh, a lead panel member held Deliveroo shares while the report was being researched and written – it does highlight a desire by the British government to tackle the issues of employment regulation. The result was proposals for a seven-step plan that encourages a mixture of worker empowerment, harnessing of previous law (promoting a National Minimum Wage, for example) and organizational cooperation in the future. The report was accused of not going far enough by those who have been fighting for improvements (see the 2017 response from the IWGB: 'Dead on Arrival.'[11]) and providing little beyond encouragement for stakeholders to change their actions. The struggle over employment classification continues in the UK, as well as whether new regulation is needed or how existing implementation can be achieved.

The lack of effective regulation for gig workers does not only have to be approached by thinking of new labour law specifically for the gig economy. Instead, one solution being discussed by the ILO (2019: 39) is the call for two 'universal labour guarantees' for all:

(a) fundamental workers' rights: freedom of association and the effective recognition of the right to collective bargaining and freedom from forced labour, child labour and discrimination; and
(b) a set of basic working conditions: (i) 'adequate living wage';[12] (ii) limits on hours of work; and (iii) safe and healthy workplaces.

The idea here is that 'all workers, regardless of their contractual arrangement or employment status, must equally enjoy adequate labour protection to ensure humane working conditions for everyone' (ILO, 2019: 38). Rather than seeking to update laws to deal with each new contractual permutation in the gig economy, this solution instead reasserts the rights of all workers. Drawing on these ideas, we – along with our colleagues Sandra Fredman, Darcy du Toit, Richard Heeks, Jean-Paul van Belle, Abigail Osiki and Paul Mungai – have produced a broad outline of a Convention on Platform Work, incorporating the Fairwork principles, which can be found in the Appendix.

Future #3: Worker power

While we need transparency in production networks and knowledge about the ways in which platform work is pieced together and governed; and while we also need genuine protections for workers and the ability for urban, regional, national and transnational regulatory bodies to hold them to account – what is really needed for genuine positive change is for platform workers to have, create and take more power in their collective destinies.

Workers in the gig economy have potential 'associational power' (Silver, 2003). This power comes from the ability of workers, brought together at work, to act collectively in their interests. This is often thought of as something that happens through unions, but it can also include campaigns, political parties or other kinds of organizations. While the gig economy has changed many of the processes at work, it still involves the buying and selling of workers' time. Workers enter into work at a structural disadvantage: they

Figure 7 Worker power

Illustration by John Philip Sage

need to sell their time to earn a living, but have very little bargaining power as individuals. However, work brings together workers – whether in factories, or increasingly now on the same streets, waiting outside the same restaurants, or communicating together on the same websites – with common interests. Often these interests can turn into shared grievances and complaints. In chapter 4, we began to sketch out these formative moments of associational power being recognized and flexed – often starting on WhatsApp or face-to-face where workers' paths cross.

While most individual workers have next to no effective bargaining power, platform workers have the power to cause massive disruption to economies and cities should they choose to collectively withdraw their labour. Imagine cities without on-demand taxis, food delivery, platform-based care work, and the myriad digital services offered by cloudworkers (often we would not realize the effect this would have until it happened). Life would go on, but it would no longer be business as usual. Some types of workers (such as drivers) even have the power to affect non-users of platforms. In cities around the world, they have blocked roads as part of their protests.

One of the problems is that workers' interests can be set against each other during periods of strikes or protests. For example, transport platforms can offer increased surge pricing or boosts to greatly increase pay rates. The often anonymous nature of the work means that the traditional picket line outside of a workplace can be harder to enforce, with other workers continuing to work on the platform. If gig economy workers are to build a better future as allies, collaborators and colleagues rather than competitors, and if they are to ever exert any effective collective power, what best practices, successes and visions should we look towards?

First, we at a minimum need strategies and platforms that can support more effective horizontal communication between workers. It is worth recalling here that most gig platforms are – at most – designed for workers to speak to their clients. Very few offer the affordances for workers to speak with one another. But, because most people in most jobs want to be able to speak to people in similar working conditions, gig economy workers from around the world have found ways of connecting. Most of these efforts occur within corporately owned tools that can be repurposed for worker organizing around the world. From Uber drivers in India to package delivery riders in South Africa, and from food delivery riders in the UK to online freelancers in the Philippines, Facebook and WhatsApp groups are the channels of choice for workers who wish to speak to one another.

On a Facebook group for Kenyan freelancers who work on platforms like Upwork and Freelancer.com, there are frequent posts by people selling each other computers, sharing news, and asking for advice. On WhatsApp groups used by delivery riders in the UK, workers post jokes and memes to pass some of the idle time while waiting for work, but also share tips on how to increase earnings. In all cases, what we are seeing is people refusing to accept the idea that they are atomized workers, and refusing to accept the idea that connectivity only runs vertically rather than horizontally. Even if workers like drivers and domestic workers rarely if ever see each other, they can start to collectively challenge ways of structuring the work processes that they are enrolled in.

The Turkopticon project is probably the most successful initiative to do this. Started in 2008, the platform allows Amazon Mechanical Turk workers to see and submit client reviews. Because wage theft is such an endemic problem on Mechanical Turk, Turkopticon found an important use amongst workers seeking to avoid some of the worst culprits. As of 2018, the platform hosted over 420,000 reviews of over 59,000 requesters. The benefit of Turkopticon is that it is integrated into the workflow of Mechanical Turk workers. However, there have also been a range of suggestions floated for worker-run, or at least worker-oriented communication platforms. Often these are additional programs or apps for workers to use. There are risks with using a platform like WhatsApp or Facebook, as they are not designed for worker organizing and lack safeguards against management surveillance or infiltration. While alternatives have their benefits, the real challenge in encouraging their use will be getting people to switch away from existing channels like Facebook and WhatsApp which rely on network effects to keep people using them. If the majority of the people you already want to speak to use Facebook and WhatsApp, then it is always going to be hard to switch an entire network to another platform.

Our discussion thus far has focused on the technologically mediated ways that workers communicate with one another. This is because, for many job types, there is simply no convergence in time and space that happens between groups of workers. But this is not always the case. In large cities, cloudworkers meet in co-working spaces and social meetup events. In many parts of the world, app-based taxi drivers congregate in places like malls and airports whilst waiting for rides. Co-presence is especially common for delivery riders who tend to have long stretches of wait-time in front of clusters of restaurants, shops and off-licences.

It is likely no coincidence that it is delivery or taxi platform workers that have had the most success in collectively organizing around the world. When the IWGB organizes Deliveroo riders and Uber drivers in the UK, The Movement organizes taxi drivers in South Africa,[13] or different unions mobilize across India, collective organization has been built on workers convening in the same times and spaces.

This brings us to our second point. Once workers have first established a foundation upon which they can effectively communicate and coordinate, we can then look to successful efforts to collectively organize and bargain. In some cases, this means workers setting up or joining official trade unions. But, in others, many workers seek to set up groups that fulfil many of the same functions of unions without the official designation.[14]

Once these groups of gig workers are established in either existing unions, new unions or groups that don't call themselves unions, they can engage in an eye-level discussion with platforms in a way that is impossible for individual workers to conduct. In Denmark, the 3F trade union signed an agreement on behalf of domestic workers with the platform Hilfr.dk that allows workers to be reclassified as employees after they have performed over 100 hours of work (Hilfr, 2018).[15] It also grants these workers an hourly minimum wage of 141 DKK (US$21) and the right to unemployment benefits and holidays, and protection against unfair dismissal.

Importantly for domestic workers, it also obliges customers to pay half the agreed wage if jobs are cancelled without sufficient notice.

The platform economy is not the only area where workers have faced precarious contracts, as we have argued in this book, both historically and in other sectors. Within the entertainment industries (as we mentioned with the origins of the term), there has been a long history of gig work. From a more recent example, the International Arts and Entertainment Alliance (IAEA) is the global union that represents workers in the Arts and Entertainment sector, bringing together three global federations. It has organized a campaign to reach out to 'atypical workers'. This involved developing 'fundamental principles and rights at work [that] apply to all workers in the media and culture sector, regardless of the nature of their employment relationship' (ILO, 2014: 25). Rather than seeing the contracts themselves as the problem – with many workers engaged in project-based work – this focuses on how to improve the rights of workers in a way that works for them within the industry. One of the member federations of the IAEA, the Media, Entertainment and Arts division of UNI, negotiates framework conditions for workers on this basis.

Similarly, in 2002 the Screen Actors Guild (SAG), which later merged with the American Federation of Television and Radio Artists to become SAG-AFTRA, passed the Global Rule 1. This required members 'to ensure that a producer is a SAG signatory and to get a SAG contract wherever they work in order to get the protections of SAG's agreements, even when working outside of the United States'.[16] This acted as a starting point to drive up working conditions, both in the US and more widely. While there are many challenges for understanding how workers and trade unions can cooperate across national boundaries and jurisdictions, positive examples like this can be taken as inspiration.

What is needed here is more visibility about the ways in which collective bargaining can be successful. Indeed, the terms and conditions offered by platforms should be seen as a starting point for negotiation rather than something that workers need to take or leave. Of course, underpinning any negotiation must be the ability for workers to collectively withdraw their labour. This is our third point. Across our fieldwork we have heard stories of workers striking and winning local concessions, often without any coverage in the media. Below the surface changes are beginning to happen in the gig economy. These stories need to be heard much more widely.

In summary, there are multiple pathways to worker power. As a start, gig economy workers need visibility. They need to be able to see and communicate with fellow workers, and they need physical places and digital networks that are conducive to building deeper collaborations. Those collaborations might happen through small and nimble local unions, groups of workers that refuse to call themselves a union, big tent domestic unions, international union federations like UNI Global, or unions like the Industrial Workers of the World. What matters is simply that gig economy workers find ways of collective bargaining, and that they are able to build the associational power, symbolic power and structural power that would be required to collectively withdraw their labour should they need to. Platforms design their digital connectivity to atomize their workforce and reduce potentials for disruption, but workers can make use of alternative connectivities to push for better working conditions. The roots of the trade union movement lie in trying to get rid of harms in the workplace, and it is possible that the rise of the gig economy will serve as a call to arms for unions and associations to build new solidarities and new strategies to improve the nature of work.

Future #4: Democratic ownership

Throughout this book we have explored the ways in which the current model of platforms is creating many negative outcomes for workers. So far in this chapter we have discussed the ways that workers are beginning to shape and reshape gig work in their own interests. In all of these cases, we see workers pushing back against the owners and managers of platforms. However, in none of the cases do we see a situation in which workers are ever truly taking

Figure 8 Democratic ownership
Illustration by John Philip Sage

control over the means of production or distribution. In this final section, we therefore wish to explore potential ways to do just that.

At the core of the platform cooperative idea is the fact that platforms operate as mediators: bringing together workers and customers. In the process, they take a substantial cut of the transactions – sometimes as high as 30 per cent. However, once the infrastructure has been set up, these platforms essentially become rent-seeking. Rather than providing anything new to either party using the platform, they collect a cut of other people's work, often driving down wages to do so. As the costs of producing apps used by platforms have fallen dramatically over time, they are no longer the sole preserve of multi-billion-dollar companies. Trebor Scholz (2017b: 47), who argues for 'platform cooperatives' (platforms that are democratically governed and cooperatively owned), proposes an alternative model for the gig economy that begins with a thought experiment:

> Just for one moment imagine that the algorithmic heart of any of these citadels of anti-unionism could be cloned and brought back to life under a different ownership model, with fair working conditions, as a humane alternative to the free market model.

The idea here is that the centuries-old cooperative model can be updated for the gig economy: drivers could come together to make and run their own taxi app, cleaners their own cleaning app, and translators their own translation app. By pooling their resources – and perhaps with the help of politically sympathetic software developers – they could start their own platform and keep more of any income taken from the client, and have more of a say of how their work is carried out. The idea has been promoted by Trebor Scholz and the Platform Cooperative Consortium based in New York.[17] The major strength of this project is that it presents an imaginary for how platform work could be organized differently. In fact, as Scholz (2017b: 50) has reiterated, 'the inability to imagine a different life is capital's ultimate triumph'. The idea of platform cooperatives connects this different vision of digital work to the long history of cooperatives: the Mondragon Corporation in the Basque Country, the long history of cooperatives in the UK, or even the example of workers taking over struggling factories and running them as successful cooperatives in countries like Greece[18] or Argentina.[19] In the current context of low-paid work in which many people have little control, just pointing out that there is a (potentially) viable alternative model for running platforms is a huge step forward. And, indeed, the platform.coop website now lists over 300 platform coops around the world who are actively trying to put into practice this alternative model for the gig economy.

While getting rid of the boss is, without doubt, an exciting idea for many workers in the gig economy (it is, after all, one of the main reasons people choose platform work), there remain inescapable economic pressures for cooperatives. This risk is acknowledged by Scholz, who notes 'the problem of competition with global corporations that are rolling in money' (Scholz, 2017b: 47). For example, a worker-owned alternative to Uber would still have to contend with Uber (and, remember, that Uber currently operates at a massive loss), regardless of how well it was structured internally. While we could hope that the millions of users in a city like New York or Johannesburg might choose to move onto a new platform that upheld workers' rights, at a more basic level there is the challenge of effectively advertising with little or no budget. After all, no one will choose the worker-friendly version of Uber if they have never heard of it. Many of these companies not only take a cut of existing transactions, but also drive down wages to unsustainably low levels. If a platform cooperative for taxis was established, you would hope the drivers would earn a decent wage. However, they would still need to operate and survive in a deeply competitive environment.

Platform cooperatives are not the only way that we could imagine a more democratic and equitable system to govern platform work. We could also think about platforms as a civic utility: the platform as a local infrastructure similar to how internet, electricity or public transport is managed in much of the world. The network effects at play in the platform economy already mean that it is unviable to have more than a few platforms focusing on the same industry in any given city. Because of these inevitable monopolistic tendencies, platforms could be regulated in a similar way to many public utilities: placing priorities such as decent jobs, environmental and social impact as necessary conditions for a licence to operate.

This idea could even be taken one step further by thinking about platforms as publicly owned and run utilities. For instance, why not find a way to have a taxi platform or a delivery platform not run by a private company with its headquarters on the other side of the world, but instead by an organization with local priorities baked into its DNA? The platform as a locally run, locally managed, and locally owned utility.

We could envisage a city setting up a ride-hailing platform, owned and managed by the city government. If we use the logic of the platform company here: this is not about a city starting, say, a taxi company; this is about a city providing opportunities for tens of thousands of drivers. It is the city (or the state, region or country) establishing a civic monopoly over the platform. Through this civic monopoly, it could ensure that decent work is the starting point for any services offered. To the end user, does it really matter if you hail a car from a city-run platform or from a privately owned one? But, to the worker, this could make a world of difference. Unlike a cooperative, this does not put the pressure on workers to offer a viable service, backing it with public resources. If it was a success, it could even cross-subsidize public transport.

There are undoubtedly significant legal and operational challenges that such organizations would face, and we shouldn't downplay those challenges. In many countries, for instance, it would be illegal for a city to set up a rival to Uber or Deliveroo. However, if we are serious about wanting new regulation to curb the damaging outcomes of platforms (Future #2), then we could also envision new regulation that facilitates and enables alternative forms of governing, organizing and managing platform work. We need to envision our desired end states that have the rights of workers and democratic ownership and governance at their core, and then work backwards from those visions. Once we do that, these alternative futures appear much more achievable.

What can you do?

Technology alone has not brought about the gig economy, and there is nothing inevitable about its current or future state. For these reasons, it is important to not just reflect on what the gig economy is and where it comes from, but also to present a series of more desirable futures. More transparency and accountability, more worker-friendly regulation, greater structural power for workers, and the democratic ownership of platforms are all futures that help to build each other. No single one of these futures alone will likely bring about meaningful change in the quality of platform jobs. What use, for instance, would the democratic ownership of platforms be, if there is no transparency about working conditions, little worker-friendly regulation and no collective body representing workers? It would likely only bring about a situation in which local government ends up running a platform for low-paid, precarious and dangerous jobs.

If we are rethinking what the gig economy can evolve into, then we need a renewed effort to encourage all four of those futures. We need more transparency about the workings of the platform economy in order to try to impose more accountability through both pressure and regulation. To see lasting changes, we need to find ways to foster, build and support the structural power of workers. And, if we want lasting and sustainable organizations committed to equitable and fair outcomes, we need to embed that power, and focus that regulation, on building more democratic institutions that occupy key nodes of information exchange in the digital economy.

Multiple gig economy models have emerged, ranging from general online freelancing platforms, which are necessarily limited in the amount of control that they can exert on work, to transportation and care work platforms, which are characterized by extremely high levels of explicit coordination and power asymmetry. But what all gig economy models have in common is a defining logic that seeks to shift maximal risk and minimal reward onto workers. Platform companies achieve this through technologies and infrastructures of connectivity that allow work to be organized via two-sided markets, political environments that impose few regulations, a zeitgeist that values flexibility, and a backdrop of increasing inequality that leads ever more workers to make the calculation that a bad job is better than no job.

The gig economy is big, and around the world there are powerful interests who only seek to make it bigger. Yet nothing about the gig economy is inevitable. If we want to make sure that we avoid yet another industry in yet another place becoming organized by the logics of the gig economy, then we all have a part to play in resisting some of its worst characteristics. What, then, can we all do?

As a start, we can begin by revisiting part of the International Labour Organization's (1944) Declaration of Philadelphia: 'labour is not like an apple or a television set, an inanimate product that can be negotiated for the highest profit or the lowest price. Work is part of everyone's daily life and is crucial to a person's dignity, well-being and development as a human being.'[20] While using an app to order a driver, a takeaway, a cleaner, a babysitter or a dog walker can remove the need to ever speak to, or meaningfully interact with, the person performing that service, a crucial first step to decommodifying work is to get to know each other, to ask questions about the people and the processes that we are interacting with, to never take the work that someone is doing for us for granted, and not to treat it as a commodity that we are buying. It is from that foundation that we can build the solidarities needed to bring about lasting change.

If we are committed to learning about the processes that we are all embedded into, then we must also be committed to adjusting our own behaviours to support some practices and avoid others. This is not about launching individual boycotts and imagining that you can change the world alone. It is rather about acting out our responsibilities to those that we are connected to and impact upon. In practice, this could mean avoiding companies engaged in some of the most egregious violations in order to be part of an economic disincentive for them doing so. But this is not just about individual actions. For strikes and boycotts to be effective, we need to collectively respect them. In other words, don't cross picket lines! If the delivery drivers in your city are on strike for higher pay, do not use the app. Platforms will continue to ignore the demands of workers if their strikes are seen as being ineffective. So help to make those strikes effective. We can do even more though. In much the same way that some platforms use their international reach to evade local accountability, we can use that same global reach of some platforms to put pressure on them. If drivers or cleaners for a large international platform are on strike in Boston, Bangalore or Bangkok, show solidarity with them in your home town by respecting the picket. At the end of the day, striking platform workers are local actors taking on a global company. Help to give their actions some global reach.

That is only the beginning though. One of the most important things that all of us can do to change the future of work is to join a union or a worker's association. This need not be a formal traditional trade union, and indeed your job and your industry may not have one. But all unions have humble beginnings. If there is not one relevant for your job, start a chat channel for your colleagues. Get together outside of the job to discuss ways of improving your work and strategies for achieving those aims. And get in touch with already existing unions to ask them for help. They usually will. Many have resources they can share, as well as advice on how to get started. The most common concern that most people have is that it feels wasteful to spend a fraction of your already small paycheque on union dues. It's hard enough to pay the bills as it is. But this is again where we have to think about our power as a collective rather than our power as atomized individuals. Chapter 4 showed how effective it can be for workers to come together for collective action and collective bargaining. Union dues are a small price to pay for an economy in which the private sector sees labour as a partner to be negotiated with at eye level rather than an inconvenience to be dealt with on an individual basis. Even if you do not work in the gig economy, join a union. Your job may be next, and strength in numbers will be needed if work is to be reshaped into fairer directions.

Because of the problems that most gig economy unions and

workers' associations have in raising dues, a lot could be done by supporting those that are on the cutting edge of cases and conflicts that will reshape the gig economy for years to come: from the IWGB and IWW in the UK, to CLAP in France, the Transnational Courier Federation across Europe, The Movement in South Africa, the New York Taxi Worker Alliance, Rideshare Drivers United, and Gig Workers Rising in the US. Their battles in the courts are often costly and they tend not to have strike funds, so donate to their causes so that they have the opportunity to win, and the resources to keep going should they lose.

Last but not least, we need to make sure that the energy, compassion and power that can be built amongst groups of workers can transition into the domains of regulation and law. The places in which we live all have parties and politicians who claim to want to remove regulatory red tape so that they support local businesses and avoid choking off innovations that are good for everyone. These are appealing ideas; after all who wants to get left behind or left out of the digital revolution. But, as we have shown, the gig economy is a petri dish for theories of limited regulation. It is precisely within a laissez-faire approach to workers' rights that the concerns we outlined in chapter 3 take form. Platforms are not going away; we will continue to have on-demand taxis and app-based food delivery, and people will continue to innovate whether or not the workers who make it all possible have decent jobs (and, indeed, we have to ask ourselves if we want those innovations if the only way to bring them into being is on the back of indecent work). We therefore all need to look to local, regional and national political parties and politicians who stand for decent jobs and who stand up for the rights of workers. We need to vote for them, campaign for them, support them, write to them and hold them to account.

The gig economy is the battleground in a set of conflicts being waged that will determine the futures of work. You may think that your own job is safe from some of the changes described in this book, but the processes that define the gig economy could come to transform almost every type of work. The balance sheet thus far is deeply worrying, and should be a cause of concern for workers the world over. And it will continue to be a concern unless we find ways of taking what we already know about how the gig economy works and who it works for, to collectively build a more equitable and fairer future of work.

Appendix:
Draft Convention on
Platform Work

A broad outline of a Convention on platform work, incorporating the Fairwork principles, and written by: Mark Graham, Sandra Fredman, Darcy du Toit, Richard Heeks, Jamie Woodcock, Jean-Paul van Belle, Abigail Osiki and Paul Mungai.

1. **Coverage**
   a. It should cover all workers, regardless of classification. A model for this is Convention 181, which states: 'This Convention applies to all categories of workers and all branches of economic activity [except seafarers].'[1] For the avoidance of doubt, it should specify that the term 'worker' refers to everyone who provides personal services mediated by the platform, including independent contractors.

2. **Pay**
   a. All platform workers should be paid for their work regularly and in full in accordance with their agreements. Platforms should ensure that such payments are made timeously.[2]
   b. Member States should take the necessary measures to ensure all workers receive just and equitable remuneration allowing

them and families to lead an existence worthy of human dignity, supplemented, if necessary, by other means of social protection.[3]

c. After consulting with representative platform owners and platform workers' representatives, Member States should establish procedures for determining minimum remuneration for platform workers, or include platform workers in existing procedures for determining remuneration for workers.[4]

d. The level of remuneration should take into account the nature of platform work;[5] the needs of platform workers and their families, taking into account the general level of wages in the country, the cost of living, social security benefits and the relative living standards of other social groups,[6] as well as economic factors such as the desirability of attaining and maintain high levels of employment.[7]

e. Appropriate measures should be put in place to ensure the effective implementation of the provisions relating to minimum remuneration.[8]

f. Minimum remuneration must not be subject to abatement by individual agreement, nor, except with general or particular authorization of the competent authority, by collective agreement.[9]

g. Workers should be given clear and regular statements as to how their remuneration is calculated, including which components are counted in the minimum, the costs paid by the worker, how the minimum is calculated for piece-rate pay, and if the minimum is an hourly or monthly rate.[10] Workers should be given a statement which sets out, in an appropriate, verifiable and easily understandable manner, the remuneration, method of calculation and periodicity of payments.[11]

3. **Health and Safety**

a. 'Workplace' covers all places where workers need to be or go by reason of their work and over which the platform has direct or indirect control or is in a position to influence by contract or otherwise.[12]

b. Where the worker works at home, national laws and regulations on health and safety must apply, taking account of its special characteristics.[13]

c. The enforcement of laws concerning occupational safety and health and the working environment for platform workers must be secured by an adequate system of inspection.[14]

d. Representatives of platform workers must be given adequate information by the platform on health and safety; workers and their representatives should be given appropriate training in relevant occupational health and safety; and should be consulted to determine their health and safety concerns.[15]

e. Adequate compensation in case of occupational accidents or diseases should be provided as and where appropriate,[16] either directly by the State or by compulsory insurance to be taken out by platforms.

f. Workers who remove themselves from a work situation which they have reasonable justification to believe presents an imminent and serious danger to their life or health must be protected from penalties.[17]

g. Employers should provide, where necessary, adequate protective clothing and protective equipment to prevent, so far as reasonably practicable, risk of accidents or adverse effects on health.[18]

h. Occupational health and safety measures must not involve any expenditure for workers.[19]

4. Hours of Work

a. Platforms should not be permitted to require or allow workers to work more than 48 hours a week, with a maximum of 8 hours a day, in order to achieve the level of wages referred to in paragraph 3(b).[20] Hourly earnings should be sufficient to make this possible. If they are not, this will breach the principle that they should not be required to work more than the maximum weekly hours.[21]

b. Workers may only be permitted to work a limited number of additional hours above the maximum and at a higher rate of earnings.

5. **Contracts**
   a. In recognition of the risk that there can be attempts to disguise the employment relationship, and that contractual arrangements can have the effect of depriving workers of the protection they are due,[22] there should be a legal presumption that an employment relation exists where one or more relevant indicators is present.
   b. Such indicators should include the fact that, expressly or in effect, the work: is carried out according to the instructions and under the control of the platform; involves the integration of the worker in the activity or the business of the platform; is performed solely or mainly for the benefit of the platform; must be carried out personally by the worker; is of a particular duration or has a certain continuity; requires the worker's availability; or involves the provision of tools, materials and machinery by the platform.[23]
   c. Platform workers should be supplied with a written statement of terms and conditions of work which clearly state all the terms of the contract.[24] Platform workers should be informed of their terms and conditions of work in an appropriate, verifiable and easily understandable manner. This should state at the very least the name and address of the other contracting party or parties, who must be subject to the local jurisdiction; remuneration, method of calculation and periodicity of payments, and terms and conditions relating to termination, including deactivation or other penalties, whether temporary or permanent.[25]
   d. Adequate procedures should be in place to investigate complaints, alleged abuses and other practices of the platform.[26]
   e. Platform workers' terms and conditions of work must be agreed to by the platform worker under conditions which ensure that the platform worker has an opportunity to review and seek advice on the terms and conditions in the agreement and freely consents before accepting.[27]

6. **Non-discrimination and Equality**
   a. Platforms should ensure that all workers are not subjected to discrimination directly or indirectly on the basis of race, colour, sex, religion, political opinion, national extraction, social origin, or any other form of discrimination covered by national law and practice, such as age or disability.[28]
   b. Platforms should protect workers against discrimination by customers or users by excluding requirements which have the effect of discriminating directly or indirectly against workers on any of the grounds mentioned in a.
   c. Equality of treatment should be promoted in relation to remuneration, statutory social security protection, minimum age for admission to employment and maternity protection.[29]
   d. Workers should have access to information explaining any decision, including the criteria for automated decisions, affecting their access to work through the platform or the terms and conditions for the performance of work.

7. **Data**
   a. Processing of data by platforms should protect workers' personal data, ensure respect for workers' privacy, and be limited to matters related to the qualification and professional experience of workers and any other directly relevant information.[30] Data should only be collected with express and informed consent of the worker and should not be shared with third parties under any circumstances without the worker's express and informed consent.

8. **Representation**
   a. Platform workers should enjoy freedom of association and the effective recognition of the right to representation and to collectively negotiate on any terms and conditions affecting their work.[31]
   b. Platform workers should have the right to establish or join organizations of their own choosing and to participate in the activities of such organizations.[32]

c. Platform workers should be adequately protected against acts of discrimination or any detrimental treatment based on their exercise of the right to freedom of association or collective representation.[33]

Notes

Introduction

1 Armstrong, S. (2017) The NHS is going to trial a gig economy app for nurses. Wired, 3 October. Available at: https://www.wired.co.uk/article/nhs-app-nurses-flexible-working-jeremy-hunt-gig-economy

2 For examples of some of our research on this topic, see Graham and Shaw (2017), Graham et al. (2017a, 2017b), Waters and Woodcock (2017), Graham and Anwar (2018, 2019), Graham and Woodcock (2018), Wood et al. (2018, 2019a, 2019b) and Woodcock (forthcoming).

3 For more on the research project, see Graham et al. (2017c) and Graham and Anwar (2018).

Chapter 1: Where did the gig economy come from?

1 https://www.wired.com/2013/12/uber-surge-pricing/

2 See https://www.itu.int/osg/csd/stratplan/AR2008_web.pdf

3 See https://www.itu.int/en/ITU-D/Statistics/Documents/facts/ICT FactsFigures2017.pdf

4 See https://www.change.org/p/save-your-uber-in-london-saveyour uber

5 The 'refusal of work' formed an important component of Italian workerism. As Bifo has argued: 'refusal of work does not mean so much the obvious fact that workers do not like to be exploited, but something more. It means that the capitalist restructuring, the technological change, and the general transformation of social institutions are produced by the daily action of withdrawal from exploitation, of rejection of the obligation to produce surplus value, and to increase the value of capital, reducing the value of life.' See http://www. republicart.net/disc/realpublicspaces/berardi01_en.htm

6 https://www.koreatimes.co.kr/www/biz/2018/08/367_253635. html

7 https://www.bls.gov/news.release/conemp.nr0.htm

Chapter 2: How does the gig economy work?

1 See https://www.gov.uk/employment-status/selfemployed-contractor

2 Employment law in the UK is slightly different, with three different employment categories, including 'the intermediate, but distinct, "worker" status [which] has entitlements to the National Minimum Wage, protection against unlawful wage deductions, statutory minimum rest breaks and paid holidays, a limit on 48 hours of work on average per week (although worker can opt out), as well as protections against discrimination and for whistleblowing'. See https:// www.gov.uk/employment-status/worker

3 See https://assets.publishing.service.gov.uk/media/5a046b06e5274a 0ee5a1f171/Uber_B.V._and_Others_v_Mr_Y_Aslam_and_Others_ UKEAT_0056_17_DA.pdf

4 See https://www.sec.gov/Archives/edgar/data/1543151/00011931 2519103850/d647752ds1.htm

5 See https://dictionary.cambridge.org/dictionary/english/uberize

6 For 'the knowledge', prospective drivers must learn over 45,000 road names and points of interest in a six-mile radius drawn around Charing Cross in London. To pass the tests (known as appearances), drivers must be able to rapidly compute a route between any given two points in order to pass.

7 See https://www.crunchbase.com/organization/uber/funding_rou nds/funding_rounds_list

8 See Isaac, M. (2017) How Uber deceives the authorities worldwide. *The New York Times*, 3 March. Available at: https://www.nytimes. com/2017/03/03/technology/uber-greyball-program-evade-auth orities.html

9 See https://www.sfgate.com/technology/businessinsider/article/ Billionaire-hedge-fund-manager-says-Uber-told-him-6271449.php

10 The taxi medallion is a system of transferable permits used in many US cities. See https://www.washingtonpost.com/news/wonk/wp/ 2014/06/20/taxi-medallions-have-been-the-best-investment-in-am erica-for-years-now-uber-may-be-changing-that/?noredirect=on& utm_term=.5c7c10ad134a

11 See https://www.uber.com/newsroom/bits-atoms-2

12 The role of machine learning as an instrument of labour control is also worth noting. Uber admits that its 'Marketplace team leverages a variety of spatiotemporal forecasting models that are able to predict where rider demand and driver-partner availability will be at various places and times in the future. Based on forecasted imbalances between supply and demand, Uber systems can encourage driver-partners ahead of time to go where there will be the greatest opportunity for rides.' https://eng.uber.com/scaling-michelangelo/

13 Because of Uber's reliance on venture capital, it is also worth noting not just the economic power that AI gives the company, but also the rhetorical power to promise to be profitable in the future.

14 See https://www.forbes.com/sites/kashmirhill/2014/10/03/god-view-uber-allegedly-stalked-users-for-party-goers-viewing-pleasure/ #75d855d03141

15 See https://techcrunch.com/2017/06/21/ubers-toxic-culture-risks-its-driverless-future-too/

16 That said, there are a few types of geographically tethered work which are essentially unrecognizable from traditional work processes. The South African platform M4JAM, for instance, pays workers to collect price data on products from nearby shops and supermarkets.

17 The argument in this section is expanded on in more detail in Graham and Anwar (2018).

18 Graham and Anwar (2019) show that 'Globally, less than seven percent of people who register for jobs are ever able to secure one.' There is, however, significant regional variation in success rates.

19 For more on the index, see https://ilabour.oii.ox.ac.uk/online-labour-index/. It is worth noting that the index ignores non-English-speaking platforms and is therefore only a selective picture of 'online labour'.

20 See World Trade Organization (2018) *World Trade Report 2018. The Future of World Trade: How Digital Technologies Are Transforming Global Commerce.* Available at: https://www.wto.org/english/res_e/publica tions_e/world_trade_report18_e.pdf

21 Quoted in Solon (2018).

22 Not only do workers have no ability to individually set rates, but they sometimes do not even know in advance what the rates that they are accepting will be.

Chapter 3: What is it like to work in the gig economy?

1 Mumit, like the names of the gig workers that will be mentioned subsequently in the book, is a pseudonym, chosen to protect their identity.

2 See https://www.thenation.com/article/best-friend-lost-life-gig-economy/

3 See https://www.arre.co.in/social-commentary/zomato-rider-reac tion-twitter-delivery-boy/

4 1 rupee equals around US$0.014, meaning 60 rupees is around US$0.86, and 30 rupees is around US$0.43.

5 See https://www.wired.co.uk/article/uber-employment-lawsuit-gig-economy-leigh-day

6 See https://www.judiciary.uk/wp-content/uploads/2016/10/aslam-and-farrar-v-uber-reasons-20161028.pdf

7 See https://www.wired.co.uk/article/uber-employment-lawsuit-gig-economy-leigh-day

8 See https://www.iol.co.za/capetimes/news/taxi-driver-hijacked-in-grassy-park-18801688

9 See https://www.news24.com/SouthAfrica/News/uber-drivers-death-raises-fears-tension-20170722

10 See https://www.timeslive.co.za/news/south-africa/2018-07-04-this-is-why-im-striking--uber-driver-explains-how-petrol-hikes-ha ve-nearly-crippled-him/

11 See Beres, D. (2014) What does it take to earn $90,000 as an Uber driver? *Huffington Post*, 4 December. Available at: https://www.huff ingtonpost.com/2014/12/04/uber-driver_n_6249608.html

12 See https://www.wired.co.uk/article/uber-employment-lawsuit-gig-economy-leigh-day

13 See Doward, J. (2018) Uber drivers '£18,000 poorer' as firm appeals two-year-old tribunal order. *The Guardian*, 28 October. Available at: https://www.theguardian.com/technology/2018/oct/28/uber-drivers-owed-thousands-in-holiday-and-sick-pay

14 See https://ig.ft.com/uber-game/

15 See https://www.theguardian.com/commentisfree/2018/apr/26/gig-economy-flexibility-exploitation-record-employment-low-wa ges-zero-hours

16 See Capetalk (2016) [LISTEN] How much does Sweepsouth pay its domestic workers? Capetalk, 27 February. Available at: http://www.capetalk.co.za/articles/293620/listen-how-much-does-sweepsouth-pay-its-domestic-workers

17 Wood et al. (2019a) show that cloudworkers, for instance, spend an average of 16 hours per week just looking for work. Which is almost 40 per cent of the time that the average cloudworker spends working!

18 Quoted in Semuels (2018).

19 Limer, E. (2014) My brief and curious life as a Mechanical Turk. Gizmodo, 28 October. Available at: https://gizmodo.com/my-brief-and-curious-life-as-a-mechanical-turk-1587864671

20 Shontell, A. (2013) When Amazon employees receive these one-character emails from Jeff Bezos, they go into a frenzy. *Business Insider*, 10 October. Available at: https://www.businessinsider.com/amazon-customer-service-and-jeff-bezos-emails-2013-10?IR=T

21 Dynamo (2014) Dear Jeff Bezos. Available at: http://www.wearedy namo.org/dearjeffbezos

22 See http://www.wearedynamo.org/dearjeffbezos

23 https://www.freelancer.com/about

24 Despite having one of the smallest GDPs in the world (129th in

2017), Palestine is the world's 50th largest destination for online freelancing work.

Chapter 4: How are workers reshaping the gig economy?

1 See Roberts, Y. (2018) The tiny union beating the gig economy giants. *The Guardian*, 1 July. Available at: https://www.theguard ian.com/politics/2018/jul/01/union-beating-gig-economy-giants-iwgb-zero-hours-workers

2 See   https://en.labournet.tv/riders-across-europe-unite-form-trans national-federation-couriers

3 See Moyer-Lee, J. (2018) When will 'gig economy' companies admit that their workers have rights? *The Guardian*, 14 June. Available at: https://www.theguardian.com/commentisfree/2018/jun/14/gig-economy-workers-pimlico-plumbers-employment-rights

4 See https://www.medianama.com/2017/05/223-tanveer-pasha-ola-uber-drivers-association/

5 See   https://www.reuters.com/article/us-uber-ola-strike/uber-ola-drivers-strike-in-india-demanding-higher-fares-idUSKCN1MW 1WZ

6 Said, C. (2015) Could client poaching undercut on-demand com-panies? *San Francisco Chronicle*, 24 April. Available at: https://www.sfchronicle.com/business/article/Could-client-poaching-undercut-on-demand-6222919.php#photo-7874032

7 Quoted in Huet (2015).

8 Quoted in Said (2015).

9 Designed by the English philosopher and social theorist, Jeremy Bentham, the panopticon is an architectural design for a prison in which a single prison guard can watch all the inmates simultaneously without them knowing whether they are being watched, thus induc-ing self-regulating behaviour.

10 See Wiessner, D. (2018) US court revives challenge to Seattle's Uber, Lyft union law. Reuters, 11 May. Available at: https://www.reuters.com/article/us-uber-seattle-unions/u-s-court-revives-challenge-to-seattles-uber-lyft-union-law-idUSKBN1IC27C

Conclusion: What next for the gig economy?

1 For further information, see http://www.followthethings.com

2 See https://medium.com/@r44d/uber-the-world-s-largest-taxi-company-owns-no-vehicles-facebook-the-world-s-most-popular-media-94a15186d020

3 Despite being a large and traditional trade union with roots in metal working, IG Metall has been at the forefront of thinking about how to respond to changes to working conditions wrought by the gig economy. They have set up an Ombuds Office for German crowdworking platforms and released a set of guidelines for decent platform-based work (IG Metall, 2016).

4 See https://citizen.co.za/news/south-africa/1454013/were-a-technology-company-not-a-taxi-service-says-uber/

5 See https://www.theguardian.com/business/2016/jul/20/uber-driver-employment-tribunal-minimum-wage

6 See https://www.judiciary.uk/wp-content/uploads/2016/10/aslam-and-farrar-v-uber-employment-judgment-20161028-2.pdf

7 See https://www.fwc.gov.au/documents/decisionssigned/html/2018fwc6836.htm

8 See https://www.theguardian.com/law/2018/feb/07/couriers-carrying-blood-for-nhs-win-full-employment-rights

9 We thank Darcy du Toit for his insightful suggestions in this section.

10 In addition to whatever beneficial tax arrangements it is able to bring about.

11 See https://iwgbunion.files.wordpress.com/2017/07/iwgb-response-to-taylor-review1.pdf

12 As explained in the report 'The ILO Minimum Wage Fixing Convention, 1970 (No. 131), provides for a minimum wage, taking into consideration: (a) the needs of workers and their families, taking into account the general level of wages in the country, the cost of living, social security benefits and the relative living standards of other social groups; and (b) economic factors, including the requirements of economic development, levels of productivity and the desirability of attaining and maintaining a high level of employment. Modalities for implementation can be designed to also address piece rates and hourly pay for self-employed workers' (ILO, 2019: 60).

13 The Movement is an organization that represents Uber drivers in South Africa.

14 There are a number of reasons why workers in some places are resistant to the idea of a trade union. In parts of India, for instance, trade unions are closely linked to political parties, many of which, in turn, are linked to ethnic and religious groups. In South Africa, many workers resent paying dues to unions that they suspect might not be transparent about how those funds are spent.

15 For more on this case, see the blog post by Valerio De Stefano: http:// regulatingforglobalization.com/2018/12/10/collective-bargaining-of-platform-workers-domestic-work-leads-the-way/

16 See https://www.sagaftra.org/about/our-history/2000s

17 See https://platform.coop/

18 Following the Greek economic crash of 2011, the chemicals factory Viome became insolvent, leaving their workers without a stable source of income. The workers occupied the plant and re-opened it as a worker-run soap factory. All workers here know how to do every stage of the production process as knowledge is distributed to empower all that work there. See https://www.theguardian.com/commentisfree/2017/jul/18/cope-capitalism-failed-factory-workers-greek-workplace-control and http://www.viome.org

19 The Argentinian FaSinPat (Fábrica Sin Patrones – or Factory Without Bosses) is a worker-run factory producing ceramics, taken into worker ownership following the 2001 Argentinian crash. See https://www.newstatesman.com/south-america/2007/08/argentina-workers-movement

20 A document that went on to form a core part of the ILO's constitution.

Appendix: Draft Convention on Platform Work

1 Article 2, C181 – Private Employment Agencies Convention, 1997 (No. 181).

2 Regulations pursuant to the Maritime Convention 2006, regulation 2.2.

3 Article 11(c), C181 – Private Employment Agencies Convention, 1997 (No. 181)

4 Maritime Convention 2006, guideline B2.2.3.
5 Maritime Convention 2006, guideline B2.2.3.
6 Article 3(a), ILO Wage Fixing Convention 1970 (No.131).
7 Article 3(b), ILO Wage Fixing Convention.
8 Article 5, ILO Wage Fixing Convention.
9 Article 2, ILO Wage Fixing Convention; Article 3(2)(3), C026 – Minimum Wage Fixing Machinery Convention, 1928 (No. 26).
10 ILO guidance on how to define a minimum wage: https://www.ilo.org/global/topics/wages/minimum-wages/definition/lang--en/index.htm
11 Article 7 (e), C189 – Domestic Workers Convention, 2011 (No. 189).
12 See, mutatis mutandis, Article 3(c), Health and Safety Convention c155. (For example, the car driven by Uber drivers; or the home cleaned by domestic workers.)
13 Article 7, C177 – Home Work Convention, 1996 (No. 177).
14 Article 9, C155 – Occupational Safety and Health Convention, 1981 (No. 155).
15 Article 19, Occupational Safety and Health Convention.
16 Article 11(h), C181 – Private Employment Agencies Convention, 1997 (No. 181).
17 Article 13, Occupational Safety and Health Convention.
18 Article 15(c), Occupational Safety and Health Convention.
19 Article 21, Occupational Safety and Health Convention.
20 See: ILO Hours of Work (Industry) Convention, 1919 (No. 1); Hours of Work (Commerce and Offices) Convention, 1930 (No. 30). The aspiration should be to achieve a 40-hour working week (Forty-Hour Week Convention, 1935 c47).
21 Recommendation concerning the Employment Relationship (R198), paragraph 11(b).
22 Preamble, Recommendation concerning the Employment Relationship (R198).
23 Recommendation concerning the Employment Relationship (R198), paragraph 13(a).
24 Regulation 2.1 paragraph 1, Maritime Labour Convention 2006.
25 Article 15, Domestic Workers Convention (C189).
26 Article 7, Domestic Workers Convention (C189).

27 Regulation 2.1 paragraph 2, Maritime Labour Convention 2006.

28 Paragraph 5(1), Private Employment Agencies Convention, 1997 (No. 181).

29 Article 4(2), Homeworkers Convention C177.

30 Article 6, ILO Convention 181.

31 C087 – Freedom of Association and Protection of the Right to Organise Convention, 1948 (No. 87); C098 – Right to Organise and Collective Bargaining Convention, 1949 (No. 98).

32 Article 2, Convention 87 Freedom of Association Convention; Article 4(a), Homeworkers Convention, c177.

33 Article 2, Convention 87 Freedom of Association Convention; Article 4(a), Homeworkers Convention, c177.

References

Aloisi, A. (2018) Dispatch No. 13 – Italy – '*With great power comes virtual freedom*': A review of the first Italian case holding that (food-delivery) platform workers are not employees. *Comparative Labor Law and Policy Journal*, https://cllpj.law.illinois.edu/dispatches

Amabile, T.M. (1983) The social psychology of creativity: A componential conceptualization. *Journal of Personality and Social Psychology*, 45(2): 357–76.

Anderson, B. (2000) *Doing the Dirty Work? The Global Politics of Domestic Labour*. London: Zed Books.

Antunes, R. (2013) *The Meanings of Work: Essays on the Affirmation and Negation of Work*. Chicago, IL: Haymarket Books.

Badger, A. (2018) Reflections on writing conspiracy theories. *The Invisible Worker*, issue 1. Available at: https://theinvisibleworker.wordpress.com/reflections-on-writing-conspiracy-theories-by-adam-badger/

Balaram, B., Warden, J. and Wallace-Stephens, F. (2017) *Good Gigs: A Fairer Future for the UK's Gig Economy*. London: RSA.

Barbrook, R. and Cameron, A. (1996) The Californian ideology. *Science as Culture*, 6(1): 44–72.

Beck, U. (1992) *Risk Society: Towards a New Modernity*. London: Sage.

Benson, A., Sojourner, A. and Umyarov, A. (2015) 'Can reputation discipline the gig economy? Experimental evidence from an online labor market', IZA DP No. 9501. Available at: http://ftp.iza.org/dp9501.pdf

Bent, P. (2017) Historical perspectives on precarious work: The cases of Egypt and India under British imperialism. *Global Labour Journal*, 8(1): 3–16.

Berg, J., Furrer, M., Harman, E., Rani, U. and Silberman, M.S. (2018) *Digital Labour Platforms and the Future of Work: Towards Decent Work in the Online World*. Geneva: ILO.

Beynon, H. (1973) *Working for Ford*. London: Allen Lane.

Binfield, K. (2004) *Luddites and Luddism*. Baltimore, MD: The Johns Hopkins University Press.

Bosch, G. (2004) Towards a new standard employment relationship in Western Europe. *British Journal of Industrial Relations*, 42(4): 617–36.

Bourdieu, P. (1998) *Contre Feux*. Paris: Raisons d'agir.

Braverman, H. (1998) *Labor and Monopoly Capital: The Degradation of Work in the Twentieth Century*. New York: Monthly Review Press.

Bruns, A. (2008) *Blogs, Wikipedia, Second Life, and Beyond: From Production to Produsage*. New York: Peter Lang.

Cant, C. (2018) The wave of worker resistance in European food platforms 2016–17. *Notes from Below*, 1. Available at: https://notesfrombelow.org/article/european-food-platform-strike-wave

Cant, C. (2019) *Riding for Deliveroo: Resistance in the New Economy*. Cambridge: Polity.

Care.com (2018) Company overview. Available at: https://www.care.com/company-overview

China Labour Bulletin (2018a) Labour relations in China: Some frequently asked questions. *China Labour Bulletin*. Available at: https://www.clb.org.hk/content/labour-relations-china-some-frequently-asked-questions

China Labour Bulletin (2018b) '@chinalabour', Twitter, 5 June. Available at: https://twitter.com/chinalabour/status/1003933538855497728?s=19

China Labour Bulletin (2018c) Didi drivers in China protest pay cuts and restrictive work practices. *China Labour Bulletin*, 3 July. Available at: https://www.clb.org.hk/content/didi-drivers-china-protest-pay-cuts-and-restrictive-work-practices

Christie, N. and Ward, H. (2018) The emerging issues for management of occupational road risk in a changing economy: A survey of gig economy drivers, riders and their managers. London: UCL Centre for Transport Studies.

Cook, I. (2004) Follow the thing: Papaya. *Antipode*, 36(4): 642–64.

Countouris, N. and De Stefano, V. (2019) *New Trade Union Strategies for New Forms of Employment*. Brussels: ETUC.

Dalla Costa, M. and James, S. (1971) *The Power of Women and the Subversion of the Community*. Brooklyn, NY: Pétroleuse Press.

De Stefano, V. (2018) A more comprehensive approach to platform-work litigation. Regulating for Globalisation, 28 November. Available at: http://regulatingforglobalization.com/2018/11/28/a-more-comp rensive-approach-to-platform-work-litigation/

Doogan, K. (2009) *New Capitalism: The Transformation of Work*. London: Polity.

du Toit, D. (2018) Uber the Border and Far Away? IR Network, LexisNexis.

Duffy, A.E.P. (1961) New unionism in Britain, 1889–1890: A reappraisal. *Economic History Review*, 14(2): 306–19.

Duménil, G. and Lévy, D. (2005) The neoliberal (counter-)revolution. In A. Saad-Filho and D. Johnston (eds.), *Neoliberalism: A Critical Reader*. London: Pluto Press.

Dynamo (2014) Dear Jeff Bezos. Available at: http://www.wearedynamo.org/dearjeffbezos

Eubanks, V. (2019) *Automating Inequality: How High-Tech Tools Profile, Police, and Punish the Poor*. New York: St. Martin's Press.

European Commission (2008) *Communication from the Commission to the European Council: A European Economic Recovery Plan*. Brussels: Commission of the European Communities.

Farr, C. (2015) Why Homejoy failed. Wired, 26 October. Available at: https://www.wired.com/2015/10/why-homejoy-failed/

Fear, C. (2018) 'Without our brain and muscle not a single wheel can turn': The IWW Couriers Network. *Notes from Below*, 3. Available at: https://notesfrombelow.org/article/without-our-brain-and-muscle

Fredman, S. (2003) Women at work: The broken promise of flexicurity. *Industrial Law Journal*, 33(4): 229–319.

Frey, C.B. and Osborne, M.A. (2017) The future of employment: How susceptible are jobs to computerisation? *Technological Forecasting and Social Change*, 114: 254–80.

Fudge, J. (2017) The future of the standard employment relationship: Labour law, new institutional economics and old power resource theory. *Journal of Industrial Relations*, 59(3): 374–92.

Gandini, A. (2016) *The Reputation Economy: Understanding Knowledge Work in Digital Society*. London: Palgrave Macmillan.

Gereffi, G., Humphrey, J. and Sturgeon, T. (2005) The governance of global value chains. *Review of International Political Economy*, 12(1): 78–104.

Goodwin, T. (2015) The Battle Is for the Customer Interface. TechCrunch, 3 March. Available at: https://techcrunch.com/2015/03/03/in-the-age-of-disintermediation-the-battle-is-all-for-the-customer-interface/

Goos, M. and Manning, A. (2007) Lousy and lovely jobs: The rising polarization of work in Britain. *Review of Economics and Statistics*, 89(1): 118–33.

Graeber, D. (2018) *Bullshit Jobs: A Theory*. London: Allen Lane.

Graham, M. and Anwar, M.A. (2018) Digital labour. In J. Ash, R. Kitchin and A. Leszczynski (eds.) *Digital Geographies*. London: Sage, pp. 177–87.

Graham, M. and Anwar, M.A. (2019) The global gig economy: Towards a planetary labour market? *First Monday*, 24(4). doi.org/10.5210/fm.v24i4.9913.

Graham, M. and Shaw, J. (eds.) (2017) *Towards a Fairer Gig Economy*. London: Meatspace Press.

Graham, M. and Woodcock, J. (2018) Towards a fairer platform economy: Introducing the Fairwork Foundation. *Alternate Routes*, 29: 242–53.

Graham, M., Hjorth, I. and Lehdonvirta, V. (2017a) Digital labour and development: Impacts of global digital labour platforms and the gig economy on worker livelihoods. *Transfer: European Review of Labour and Research*, 23(2): 135–162.

Graham, M., Lehdonvirta, V., Wood, A., Barnard, H., Hjorth, I. and Simon, D.P. (2017b) *The Risks and Rewards of Online Gig Work at the Global Margins*. Oxford: Oxford Internet Institute.

Graham, M., Ojanpera, S., Anwar, M.A. and Friederici, N. (2017c) Digital connectivity and African knowledge economies. *Questions de Communication*, 32: 345–60.

Gray, M.L. and Suri, S. (2019) *Ghost Work: How to Stop Silicon Valley from Building a New Global Underclass*. New York: Houghton Mifflin Harcourt.

Gray, M.L., Suri, S., Ali, S.S. and Kulkarni, D. (2016), The crowd is a collaborative network. In *CSCW'16: Proceedings of the 19th ACM Conference on Computer-Supported Cooperative Work & Social Computing, San Francisco, CA, 27 February–2 March*. New York: ACM Press, pp. 134–47.

Gupta, N., Martin, D., Hanrahan, B. and O'Neill, J. (2014) Turk-life in India. In *Proceedings of the ACM International Conference on Supporting Group Work (GROUP'14) Sanibel Island, 9–12 November*.

Hara, K., Adams, A., Milland, K., Savage, S., Callison-Burch, C. and Bigham, J.P. (2018) A data-driven analysis of workers' earnings on Amazon Mechanical Turk. In *CHI'18: Proceedings of the 2018 CHI Conference on Human Factors in Computing Systems*, Paper No. 449. New York: ACM Press.

Harvey, D. (1989) *The Urban Experience*. Oxford: Blackwell.

Harvey, D. (2007) *A Brief History of Neoliberalism*. Oxford: Oxford University Press.

Heeks, R. (2017) Decent work and the digital gig economy: A developing country perspective on employment impacts and standards in online outsourcing, crowdwork, etc. Paper No. 71. Manchester: Centre for Development Informatics, Global Development Institute, SEED.

Herman, S., Johnson, C., Hunter, R., Dunn, M. and Janse van Vuuren, P.F. (2019) Africa's digital platforms and financial services: An eight-country overview. Available at: https://www.i2ifacility.org/system/documents/files/000/000/086/original/DIGITAL_ADP_Focus_Note.pdf?1553833148

Heyes, J. (2011) Flexicurity, employment protection and the jobs crisis. *Work, Employment and Society*, 25(4): 642–57.

Hilfr (2018) Historic agreement: First ever collective agreement for the platform economy signed in Denmark. Available at: http://blog.hilfr.dk/en/historic-agreement-first-ever-collective-agreement-platform-economy-signed-denmark/

Hill, S. (2017) *Raw Deal: How the 'Uber Economy' and Runaway Capitalism Are Screwing American Workers*. New York: St Martin's Press.

Hochschild, A.R. (1983) *The Managed Heart: The Commercialisation of Human Feeling*. Berkeley, CA: University of California Press.

Hochschild, A.R. (1989) *The Second Shift: Working Families and the Revolution at Home*. New York: Penguin.

Howe, J. (2006) The rise of crowdsourcing. Wired, 1 May. Available at: http://www.wired.com/2006/06/crowds/

Huet, E. (2015) What really killed Homejoy? It couldn't hold on to its customers. Forbes, 23 July. Available at: https://www.forbes.com/sites/ellenhuet/2015/07/23/what-really-killed-homejoy-it-couldnt-hold-onto-its-customers/#22c9f5871874

Hunt, A. and Machingura, F. (2016) A good gig? The rise of on-demand domestic work. ODI Development Progress, Working Paper 7.

Hunt, A. and Samman, E. (2019) Gender and the gig economy. ODI Working Paper 546.

Huws, U. and Joyce, S. (2016) Crowd working survey: Size of the UK's 'gig economy'. Hatfield: University of Hertfordshire.

Huws, U., Spencer, N. and Joyce, S. (2016) Crowd work in Europe: Preliminary results from a survey in the UK, Sweden, Germany, Austria and the Netherlands. Hatfield: University of Hertfordshire.

Hyman, R. (1989) *Strikes*, 4th edn. Glasgow: Macmillan Press.

Iles, A. (2005) The insecurity lasts a long time. *Mute: Precarious Reader*, 2: 34–36.

International Labour Organization (ILO) (2011) *Policies and Regulations to Combat Precarious Employment*. Geneva: International Labour Office.

International Labour Organization (ILO) (2014) *Global Dialogue Forum on Employment Relationships in the Media and Culture Sector: Final report of the discussion*. Geneva: International Labour Office.

International Labour Organization (ILO) (2019) *Work for a Brighter Future*. Geneva: International Labour Office.

Irani, L. (2015) The cultural work of microwork. *New Media & Society*, 17(5): 720–39.

Irani, L. and Silberman, M.S. (2013) Turkopticon: Interrupting worker invisibility in Amazon Mechanical Turk. *Proceedings of CHI 2013, 28 April–2 May*.

IWGB (2018) Uber drivers to strike for 24 hours in London, Birmingham and Nottingham. IWGB, 8 October. Available at: https://iwgb.org.uk/post/5bbb3ff1bf94a/uber-drivers-to-strike-for

Jacoby, S.M. (2004) *Employing Bureaucracy: Managers, Unions, and the Transformation of Work in the 20th Century*. Mahwah, NJ: Lawrence Erlbaum.

Kaganer, E., Carmel, E., Hirscheim, R. and Olsen, T. (2013) Managing the human cloud. *MIT Sloan Management Review*, 54(2): 23–32.

Kalanick, T. (2013) Uber Policy White Paper 1.0. Uber. Available at: http://www.benedelman.org/uber/uber-policy-whitepaper.pdf

Kalanick, T. and Swisher, K. (2014) Uber CEO: We're in a political battle with an 'assh*le', Mashable, 28 May. Available at: http://mash able.com/2014/05/28/travis-kalanick-co-founder-and-ceo-of-uber/

Kalleberg, A.L. (2009) Precarious work, insecure workers: Employment relations in transition. *American Sociological Review*, 74(1): 1–22.

Kaplanis, I. (2007) *The Geography of Employment Polarisation in Britain*. London: Institute for Public Policy Research.

Kessler, S. (2018) *Gigged: The Gig Economy, the End of the Job and the Future of Work*. New York: St. Martin's Press.

Klein, N. (2008) *The Shock Doctrine*. London: Penguin Books.

Kuhn, J.W. (1961) *Bargaining in Grievance Settlement: The Power of Industrial Work Groups*. New York: Columbia University Press.

Lanier, J. (2014). *Who Owns the Future?* New York: Simon and Schuster.

Lee, M.K., Kusbit, D., Metsky, E. and Dabbish, L. (2015) Working with machines: The impact of algorithmic, data-driven management on human workers. In B. Begole, J. Kim, K. Inkpen and W. Wood (eds.), *Proceedings of the 33rd Annual ACM SIGCHI Conference*. New York: ACM Press.

McDowell, L., Batnitzky, A. and Dyer, S. (2009) Precarious work and economic migration: Emerging immigrant divisions of labour in Greater London's service sector. *International Journal of Urban and Regional Research*, 33(1): 3–25.

MacGregor, S. (2005) The welfare state and neoliberalism. In A. Saad-Filho and D. Johnston (eds.), *Neoliberalism: A Critical Reader*. London: Pluto Press.

McIlroy, J. (1995) *Trade Unions in Britain Today*. Manchester: Manchester University Press.

McKarthy, K. (2005) Is precarity enough? *Mute: Precarious Reader*, 2: 54–8.

McKinsey Global Institute (2017) Where machines could replace humans and where they can't (yet). London: McKinsey Global Institute.

Mankelow, R. (2017) The Port of London, 1790–1970. In S. Davies, C. J. Davis, D. de Vries, L.H. van Voss, L. Hesselink and K. Weinhauer (eds.), *Dock Workers: International Explorations in Comparative History, 1790–1970, Volume 1.* London: Routledge.

Manyika, J., Lund, S., Robinson, K., Valentino, J. and Dobbs, R. (2015) Connecting talent with opportunity in the digital age. McKinsey & Company. Available at: https://www.mckinsey.com/featured-insights/employment-and-growth/connecting-talent-with-opportunity-in-the-digital-age

Manyika, J., Lund, S., Bughin, J., Robinson, K., Mischke, J. and Mahajan, D. (2016), Independent work: Choice, necessity, and the gig economy. Available at: https://www.mckinsey.com/~/media/McKinsey/Featured%20Insights/Employment%20and%20Growth/Independent%20work%20Choice%20necessity%20and%20the%20gig%20economy/Independent-Work-Choice-necessity-and-the-gig-economy-Full-report.ashx

Marlow, J. (1971) *The Tolpuddle Martyrs.* London: History Book Club.

Marx, K. (1845) Theses on Feuerbach. Available at: https://www.marxists.org/archive/marx/works/1845/theses/theses.htm

Marx, K. (1955 [1847]) *The Poverty of Philosophy.* Moscow: Progress Publishers.

Marx, K. (1976) *Capital: A Critique of Political Economy Vol. 1.* London: Penguin Books.

Mason, P. (2016) *PostCapitalism: A Guide to our Future.* London: Penguin.

Massey, D. (1984) *The Spatial Divisions of Labour.* New York: Routledge.

Mitropoulos, A. (2005) Precari-Us. *Mute: Precarious Reader,* 2: 12–19.

Moody, K. (2017) *On New Terrain: How Capital is Reshaping the Battleground of Class War.* Chicago, IL: Haymarket.

Moulier-Boutang, Y. (2012) *Cognitive Capitalism.* Cambridge: Polity.

Munke, R. (2005) Neoliberalism and politics, and the politics of neoliberalism. In A. Saad-Filho and D. Johnston (eds.), *Neoliberalism: A Critical Reader.* London: Pluto Press.

Nedelkoska, L. and Quintini, G. (2018) Automation, skills use and training. OECD Social, Employment and Migration Working Papers

No. 202. Available at: https://www.oecd-ilibrary.org/employment/automation-skills-use-and-training_2e2f4eea-en

Noble, S.U. (2018) *Algorithms of Oppression: How Search Engines Reinforce Racism*. New York: NYU Press.

OECD (2019) Measuring platform mediated workers. OECD Digital Economy Papers No. 282.

Ojanperä, S., O'Clery, N. and Graham, M. (2018) Data science, artificial intelligence and the futures of work. Alan Turing Institute Report, 24 October. Available at: http://doi.org/10.5281/zenodo.1470609

O'Neil, C. (2017) *Weapons of Math Destruction: How Big Data Increases Inequality and Threatens Democracy*. London: Penguin.

Pasquale, F. (2015) *The Black Box Society: The Secret Algorithms That Control Money and Information*. Cambridge, MA: Harvard University Press.

Peck, J. (2013) Explaining (with) neoliberalism. *Territory, Politics, Governance*, 1(2): 132–57.

Peck, J. (2017) *Offshore: Exploring the Worlds of Global Outsourcing*. Oxford: Oxford University Press.

Pollert, A. and Charlwood, A. (2009) The vulnerable worker in Britain and problems at work. *Work, Employment and Society*, 23(2): 343–62.

Pollman, E. and Barry, J. (2016) Regulatory entrepreneurship. *Southern California Law Review*, 90: 383–442.

Ravenelle, A. (2019) *Hustle and Gig: Struggling and Surviving in the Sharing Economy*. Oakland, CA: University of California Press.

Raw, L. (2009) *Striking a Light: The Bryant and May Matchwomen and their Place in History*. London: Continuum Books.

Richey, L.A. and Ponte, S. (2011) *Brand Aid: Shopping Well to Save the World*. Minneapolis, MN: University of Minnesota Press.

Roberts, S.T. (2016) Commercial content moderation: Digital laborers' dirty work. In S.U. Noble and B. Tynes (eds.), *The Intersectional Internet: Race, Sex, Class and Culture Online*. New York: Peter Lang.

Rosenblat, A. (2018) *Uberland: How Algorithms are Rewriting the Rules of Work*. Oakland, CA: University of California Press.

Rosenblat, A. and Stark, L. (2016) Algorithmic labor and information asymmetries: A case study of Uber's drivers. *International Journal of Communication*, 10: 3758–84.

Ryan, B. (2005) *Labour Migration and Employment Rights*. Liverpool: Institute of Employment Rights.

Salehi, N., Irani, L.C., Bernstein, M.S., Alkhatib, A., Ogbe, E., Milland, K. and Clickhappier (2015) We are Dynamo: Overcoming stalling and friction in collective action for crowd workers. *Proceedings of CHI'2015, 18–23 April*.

Scholz, T. (2015) Think outside the boss. Public Seminar, 5 April. Available at: http://www.publicseminar.org/2015/04/think-outside-the-boss

Scholz, T. (2017a) *Uberworked and Underpaid: How Workers are Disrupting the Digital Economy*. Cambridge: Polity.

Scholz, T. (2017b) Platform cooperativism vs. the sharing economy. In N. Douay and A. Wan (eds.), *Big Data & Civic Engagement*. Rome: Planum Publisher.

Scott, W.R. (2001) *Institutions and Organizations*. Thousand Oaks, CA: Sage.

Semuels, A. (2018) The Internet is enabling a new kind of poorly paid hell. The Atlantic, 23 January, Available at: https://www.theatlantic.com/business/archive/2018/01/amazon-mechanical-turk/551192/

Silver, B.J. (2003) *Forces of Labor, Workers' Movements and Globalization since 1870*. Cambridge: Cambridge University Press.

Slee, T. (2015) *What's Yours Is Mine: Against the Sharing Economy*. London: OR Books.

Smith, A. (2016) Gig work, online selling and home sharing. Pew Research Centre, 17 November. Available at: http://www.pewinternet.org/2016/11/17/gig-work-online-selling-and-home-sharing/

Solon, O. (2018) The rise of 'pseudo-AI': How tech firms quietly use humans to do bots' work. *The Guardian*, 6 July. Available at: https://www.theguardian.com/technology/2018/jul/06/artificial-intelligence-ai-humans-bots-tech-companies

Srnicek, N. (2017) *Platform Capitalism*. Cambridge: Polity.

Standing, G. (2011) *The Precariat: The New Dangerous Class*. London: Bloomsbury.

Standing, G. (2016) *The Corruption of Capitalism: Why Rentiers Thrive and Work Does Not Pay*. London: Biteback Publishing.

Sundararajan, A. (2017) *The Sharing Economy: The End of Employment and the Rise of Crowd-Based Capitalism*. Cambridge, MA: MIT Press.

Susskind, R. (2018) AI, work and outcome-thinking. *British Academy Review*, 34: 30–1.

SweepSouth (2018) Report on pay and working conditions for domestic work in SA 2018. SweepSouth, 13 May. Available at: https://blog.sweepsouth.com/2018/05/13/report-on-pay-and-working-conditions-for-domestic-work-in-sa-2018/

Taylor, F. (1967) *The Principles of Scientific Management*. New York: Norton.

Taylor, P. and Bain, P. (2005) 'India calling to the far away towns': The call centre labour process and globalization. *Work, Employment and Society*, 19(2): 261–82.

Taylor, B. and Li, Q. (2007) Is the ACFTU a union and does it matter? *Journal of Industrial Relations*, 49(5): 701–15.

Taylor, M., Marsh, G., Nicol, D. and Broadbent, P. (2017) Good work: The Taylor Review of modern working practice. Available at: https://assets.publishing.service.gov.uk/government/uploads/system/uploads/attachment_data/file/627671/good-work-taylor-review-modern-working-practices-rg.pdf

Thompson, P. and Ackroyd, S. (1995) All quiet on the workplace front? A critique of recent trends in British industrial sociology. *Sociology*, 29: 615–33.

Tillett, B. (1910) *A Brief History of the Dockers' Union*. London: Dock, Wharf, Riverside & General Workers' Union.

Ticona, J. and Mateescu, A. (2018) Trusted strangers: Carework platforms' cultural entrepreneurship in the on-demand economy. *New Media & Society*, 20(11): 4384–404.

Tucker, J. (1993) Everyday forms of employee resistance. *Sociological Forum*, 8(1): 25–45.

van Doorn, N. (2017) Platform labor: On the gendered and racialized exploitation of low-income service work in the 'on-demand' economy. *Information, Communication & Society*, 20(6): 898–914.

Vandaele, K. (2018) Will trade unions survive in the platform economy? Emerging patterns of platform workers' collective voice and representation in Europe. Working Paper. Brussels: European Trade Union Institute.

Waters, F. and Woodcock, J. (2017) Far from seamless: A workers' inquiry at Deliveroo. *Viewpoint Magazine*, 20 September. Available at: https://www.viewpointmag.com/2017/09/20/far-seamless-workers-inquiry-deliveroo/

Webster, E., Lambert, R. and Bezuidenhout, A. (2008) *Grounding Globalization: Labour in the Age of Insecurity*. Oxford: Blackwell.

Weightman, G. and Humphries, S. (2007) *The Making of Modern London: A People's History of the Capital from 1815 to the Present Day*. London: Random House.

Williams, E. (1994) *Capitalism and Slavery*. Chapel Hill, NC: University of North Carolina Press.

Williams, S. and Adam-Smith, D. (2009) Web case: Trade unions and the prospects for unionization in the service sector. In S. Williams and D. Adam-Smith (eds.), *Contemporary Employment Relations: A Critical Introduction*, 2nd edn. Oxford: Oxford University Press.

Wood, A.J. (2015) Networks of injustice and worker mobilisation at Walmart. *Industrial Relations Journal*, 46(4): 259–74.

Wood, A.J., Lehdonvirta, V. and Graham, M. (2018) Workers of the Internet unite? Online freelancer organisation among remote gig economy workers in six Asian and African countries. *New Technology, Work and Employment*, 33(2): 95–112.

Wood, A., Graham, M., Lehdonvirta, A. and Hjorth, I. (2019a) Good gig, bad big: Autonomy and algorithmic control in the global gig economy. *Work, Employment and Society*, 33(1): 56–75.

Wood, A., Graham, M., Lehdonvirta, A. and Hjorth, I. (2019b) Networked but commodified: The (dis)embeddedness of digital labour in the gig economy. *Sociology*, https://doi.org/10.1177/0038038519828906

Woodcock, J. (2014a) The workers' inquiry from Trotskyism to Operaismo: A political methodology for investigating the workplace. *Ephemera*, 14(3): 493–513.

Woodcock, J. (2014b) Precarious work in London: New forms of organisation and the city. *City: Analysis of Urban Trends, Culture, Theory, Policy, Action*, 18(6): 776–88.

Woodcock, J. (2017) *Working the Phones: Control and Resistance in Call Centres*. London: Pluto.

Woodcock, J. (2018a) Changes in employment: Role of the state and its reconfiguration in the liberalization of employment policies. In O. Fedyuk and P. Stewart (eds.), *Inclusion and Exclusion in Europe:*

Migration, Work and Employment Perspectives. London: ECPR Press, pp. 17–34.

Woodcock, J. (2018b) Digital labour and workers' organisation. In M. Atzeni and I. Ness (eds.), *Global Perspectives on Workers' and Labour Organizations.* Singapore: Springer, pp. 157–73.

Woodcock, J. (forthcoming) The algorithmic Panopticon at Deliveroo: Measurement, precarity, and the illusion of control. *Ephemera.*

Woodcock, J. and Johnson, M.R. (2018) Gamification: What it is, and how to fight it. *The Sociological Review,* 66(3): 542–58.

Yin, M., Gray, M.L., Suri, S. and Vaughan, J.W. (2016), The communication network within the crowd. *Proceedings of the 25th International World Wide Web Conference (WWW), Montreal, Canada, 11 April.*

Index

185